GHOSTS and WITCHES APLENTY

MORE TALES OUR SETTLERS TOLD

Joseph and Edith Raskin

Illustrated by WILLIAM SAUTS BOCK

SCHOLASTIC BOOK SERVICES

NEW YORK • TORONTO • LONDON • AUCKLAND • SYDNEY • TOKYO

NOTE

All the stories in this special Arrow edition of *Ghosts and Witches Aplenty* are complete and unabridged. However, the second and fifth stories of the original hard cover edition were omitted, since they were not about ghosts or witches.

ISBN: 0-590-31944-2

Copyright © 1973 by Joseph Raskin and Edith Raskin. This abridged edition is published by Scholastic Book Services, a division of Scholastic Magazines, Inc., by arrangement with Lothrop, Lee & Shepard Company, a division of William Morrow & Company, Inc.

13 12 11 10 9 8 7 6 5 4 3 2   0 1 2 3/8

To our good friend
MATT ROCKER

CONTENTS

A Pot of Trouble

Salem — Place of Peace — was far from peaceful at the time Mary March was growing up. There were tales of ghosts and witches aplenty in those days, and no person in that Massachusetts village believed himself safe from their evil spells. The good folks were worried, and all they could do was fast and pray that they be spared from their worst enemies, the Devil and his crew.

Mary March did her share of praying, but as every sunrise promised a day of delightful happenings, she left worrying to her elders. At the age of eighteen she was a beautiful girl with a fair complexion, blue eyes, and a full mouth that was ready at any moment to curve into a merry smile. The girls of the village were jealous of her good looks, and there was no end to their envy when they heard she was marrying Willie Brown. They had good reason to be envious, for Willie Brown, in addition to being a most likable lad, was also a prosperous farmer.

"She doesn't deserve him. She is too flighty to make him a good wife," they whispered when the young couple were married.

While Mary paid little attention to the gossip that reached her ears, the unfriendly behavior of Willie's mother was a burden in her new life. Ever since her mother-in-law had become a widow, she had clung to Willie and lived in fear of losing him. Convinced that no girl was good enough to be his wife, she let Mary know in many subtle ways that she was not welcome to live in their house. Mary tried to win the older woman's love, but no matter what she did, she was met with a frown.

"Don't you go messing up the dishes in the cupboard again," the old woman scolded her after Mary had washed some and placed them on the wrong shelf.

"Did I do that?" Mary said innocently, and proceeded to rearrange them properly.

This only infuriated Mrs. Brown the more. Turning away, she muttered to herself, "I know her witching ways."

Scarcely a day went by that Mrs. Brown did not find some fault with her daughter-in-law. Mary tried to take this lightly, hoping that in time her mother-in-law would get over resenting her presence. And when Willie came home from work, she would meet him with a bright smile as if nothing unpleasant had happened during the day.

One morning, hearing that the village merchant had just received a fresh supply of cloth from Boston, Mary hurried over and bought a length of it for a dress. It was a lovely dotted pattern, a kind not seen in Salem before. Excited over her purchase and impatient to see how the material became her, Mary wrapped it around her before the mirror as soon as she got home.

"What are you up to?" Mrs. Brown demanded suspiciously.

"I am making a dress for myself. I hope Willie will like it!" Mary replied with shining eyes.

"Only a wicked woman would wear such a gaudy dress," the old woman berated her. Snatching the cloth away from Mary, she said, "I'll have to keep an eye on you to see that you behave properly."

Upset and worried, this time Mary told her husband what had happened.

"Don't pay any attention to her antics," he

laughed. "Father and I never did. Beneath her simple homespun, Mother really has a kind heart."

After the incident with the dress, Mrs. Brown rarely spoke to her daughter-in-law, instead, she spent a good deal of her time sitting at the big fireplace doggedly watching Mary out of the corner of her eye. Mary, remembering what Willie had told her, gradually accustomed herself to the old woman's behavior and went about cheerfully attending to her own chores.

One morning Mrs. Brown ventured out to see her neighbor and pick up some bits of gossip. Returning a while later, she found Mary leaning over a steaming pot hanging on the crane in the fireplace. Tiptoeing closer, she saw Mary plunge her hand into the boiling water in the pot and pull out a long white bag.

"What are you doing?" she demanded.

Startled, Mary didn't reply at once. Then as she was transferring the white bag to a pewter dish, she said with a mysterious smile, "You'll see."

The table was set and the steaming pewter dish placed on it when Willie came home for his midday meal. After the prayer was said, Mary turned to Mrs. Brown with sparkling eyes, "Now, Mother, lift the cover and see what's underneath."

As Mrs. Brown remained sitting with a frozen face, Willie obliged and lifted the cover from the dish, revealing round dumplings.

"I don't think it's pudding. And they aren't cakes," he observed, mystified. "Then what are they?"

Putting a dumpling on his plate, Mary said importantly, "Cut it open!"

Expectantly Willie cut the crust open, and behold, there was a prize — an apple inside! "Isn't this a wonderful surprise, Mother!" he exclaimed.

For a moment old Mrs. Brown silently glowered at the outlandish concoction; then she grabbed the pewter dish with the rest of the dumplings and ran out of the room.

"What's wrong, Mother?" Willie called after her. But his mother had already left the house, locking the pair inside.

Turning pale and clinging to her husband, Mary cried, "Oh, Willie, I'm afraid. She is out to do us harm."

Willie tried to laugh that off. "Frightened of Mother? Why, everybody in the neighborhood will tell you that she has the kindest heart they've ever known."

Barely an hour had passed when half the village came storming to the house, led by old Mrs. Brown. There in the crowd was the parson, praying for the sinner, and the deacons with grave faces, ready to join in denouncing whatever evil spirit might be found lurking in the house. The women were screaming threats, while the sheriff was trying to hold them back by the force of his mighty voice.

"The evil one is in there!" old Mrs. Brown shrieked, unlocking the door. "Don't let the witch escape!"

The sheriff, accompanied by some villagers, tore into the room to find Willie standing with his arm around his trembling wife.

"We want her," the sheriff demanded, pointing at Mary. "She's accused of being a witch." Seeing that Willie Brown showed no willingness to hand over his wife, the sheriff moved toward him.

"Don't you touch her. She is innocent," Willie warned him, stepping in front of his wife to protect her.

Fearing that the sheriff, encouraged by the righteous villagers, would harm Willie, Mary pleaded with her husband, "Let me go with them. They are our friends; I trust their fair judgment."

But Willie stubbornly refused to heed Mary's pleas, and violently resisted the sheriff's attempt to snatch her. Overwhelmed by sheer numbers, he was finally knocked to the ground, and Mary was led away to prison.

Leaning over her son, old Mrs. Brown prayed "Oh God forgive you, Willie." And a deacon echoed her, "Amen."

Some days later Mary was brought to court for questioning.

"You are accused of preparing a fiendish concoction," one of the judges declared. "Are you willing to confess your guilt?"

"I have nothing to confess. I am innocent, your honor," Mary replied bravely. "And it wasn't a fiendish concoction, but simply apple dumplings that I made."

The judge raised his brows. "Apple dumplings? What in God's name is that?"

"A new delicious dish, Your Honor," Mary enlightened him.

The judge shook his head doubtfully, and went into a huddle with the other judges to decide what to make of Mary's unexpected declaration. They finally decided to stage a novel trial.

The village was buzzing with excitement and people came from near and far on the day of the trial. Work was put aside and everybody donned holiday clothes. Court was being held on Willie Brown's green field close to his orchard, which on this September day was loaded with ripening apples.

By afternoon, everything was ready for the trial to begin. The parson made his way through the crowd and arranged his bulky self on the high bench. Below him Mrs. Brown took her place, along with twelve churchmen who were to proclaim the final verdict.

A huge crowd gathered in the field and watched with anticipation as an open fire was prepared and a black kettle filled with water hung over it. Their suspense was increased when a board was set up and a mound of flour, some apples, and a dish were placed on it.

Suddenly a murmur went through the crowd. "There she is! The witch!" Stretching their necks and standing on tiptoes, they tried to get a better glimpse of her.

Unruffled by their catcalls, Mary smiled to them as she advanced toward the stand. But she couldn't help noticing the sneer on the face of that pampered youth of the village whom she had refused to marry. Nor did she fail to see her envious girlfriends standing together and glowing at the prospect of the punishment to be pronounced on her.

As she rolled up her sleeves and put on an apron, a hush descended upon the field. There was not a breeze now to disturb the air, and not the slightest rustle of leaves in the orchard. Even the grasshoppers stopped their singing and seemed to join the crowd in watching.

While the crowd was merely curious, the parson and the twelve stately churchmen sitting in judgment were wholly concentrating on Mary's every move. With grave faces they watched her stir the flour into a paste and skillfully roll it out. Carefully wrapping each apple in the dough so that not a single seam showed, she then put them all in a long white bag. They gasped as they saw Mary drop the strange bag into the black pot filled with boiling water; then sitting back and folding their hands, they waited.

"Half an hour!" the parson thundered at last, holding his watch up to his eyes.

The twelve elders gathered around the black pot and, frowning, stared into its deep bottom.

"For my part, I prefer the old ways to the new," one of the elders grumbled. "The proper way to deal with a witch is to put her in a bonfire."

"That's true," another elder replied. "I too believe in the justice of our Lord and the good laws of the past. But let us be patient and reserve our judgment for the time being."

While the worthy men were thus exchanging their views, the parson himself stepped down from his high seat, armed with a pair of tongs.

With the skill of an experienced fisherman, he dipped his tongs into the boiling water and pulled out the white bag. Then carrying the steaming mess to the board, he cut the hemp string with a firm hand and rolled the dumplings into the dish.

"I watched every move of this Mary Brown," he finally announced. "There is no magic to making dumplings; I can testify to that."

The twelve elders nodded their heads in full agreement. "Of course, of course," they proclaimed.

Astonished by the verdict of not guilty, for a few moments the crowd remained silent. Presently their mood changed, and the field resounded with "Hurrah, hurrah!" And the distant hills echoed, "Hur-rah!"

Mary soon became a much respected person in Salem and was admired by all those who a short while before had considered her a witch. "We knew right along you were innocent," her girlfriends now assured her.

No longer did old Mrs. Brown sit at the fireplace spying on Mary. On the contrary, she even insisted on helping whenever Mary was making that novel dish, apple dumplings.

They Called Her a Witch

From the day Miriam Gray was born, many people of Cochichawick in the Massachusetts Colony had a foreboding that an evil spirit would direct her throughout her natural life. For still fresh in their minds was her mother's testimony at the witchcraft trial of Martha Corrier and the horrible ending of the accused on Gallows Hill in nearby Salem. Surely the condemned witch's curse on the mother would be brought to bear on the child.

Miriam was the ninth child in the Gray family and the brightest. When the schoolmaster in the old log schoolhouse asked a difficult question, she was the first to answer it. She followed the rules of proper behavior better than all the other pupils. And no one in school remembered to place his or her feet on the mark more precisely when reciting the lesson than this beautiful black-eyed girl with the little upturned nose.

At home she was the envy of her sisters. They marveled at her ease in running the great spinning wheel, spinning and knotting the linen thread to get it ready for weaving cloth in the winter months. "Almost as good as Mother," they would sigh as they watched her.

At the age of sixteen she knew as much about farming and attending to domestic animals as any farmer in the neighborhood. It amused her to see the shamed faces of her brothers when she filled up her milk pail faster than they did. The boys shrugged it off. "No wonder — she's a girl, so she has a special soft touch. When she milks Old Chestnut or High Horn, they help her finish faster."

With pride Gray watched his daughter Miriam maturing into a beautiful woman. However, the young men of the town, attracted to her though they were, heeded the warning of their parents and shunned her. "Remember, the girl's mother has a witch's curse hanging over her which might also be hanging over her daughter," they said.

At that time in Shawshine, a town twenty miles away from Cochichawick, there lived a prosperous man named Solomon Fay. His oldest son Benjamin, a handsome and energetic youth, on coming of age decided to venture out on his own. With the approval and aid of his father, he purchased the mill and the simple dwelling alongside it that stood at the stream near the town. The stream was a convenient way to travel to the mill, for there were no trodden roads between villages.

The pioneers, braving the rough stream, readily came with their crops to the mill, and there was scarcely an hour during the week when the mill wasn't grinding corn into meal for a waiting customer.

"You'd better get yourself a wife to help you," they advised the miller.

"And who'll be attending to the mill while I go off finding her?" Benjamin replied with a twinkle in his eye.

Nevertheless the people of Shawshine began to notice that on Sundays Benjamin would paddle off in his canoe and wouldn't return till dark. Could he be going off to do business on the Sabbath, they asked one another disapprovingly? One Sunday afternoon they were surprised to see a party of men and women, with Benjamin among them, landing their canoe near town.

"You've been urging me to find a wife," he

called to the townspeople who began gathering around him and his party. "Well, here she is!" he pointed at Miriam Gray.

The townspeople stared at Miriam with astonishment. She was wearing a mantle of the brightest scarlet and a broad-brimmed hat with flowing feathers to match. This bridal gift from her father, ordered from England, was meant to complement her sparkling black eyes and striking black hair. But it had a completely different effect on the townspeople.

"She must be in league with the hateful British redcoats to be wearing such a color." "This proves she is cursed, just as we heard her mother was." "Most likely she's a witch," they whispered to one another.

Unaware of the people's suspicions, Benjamin and Miriam were married the following day, and nowhere in the colonies were there two people happier than this young couple. Tirelessly Miriam went to work transforming their crude dwelling into a pleasant home, yet finding time to help her husband at the mill.

But although she was a good and faithful wife, people remained suspicious of her. They avoided coming too close to her house if they could help it, and whenever she appeared in town wearing her scarlet mantle they hurriedly shut the shutters of their windows.

Their behavior toward her didn't escape Miriam's notice. But, saddened though she was by it, she didn't complain. It was not so with Benjamin. "I'll have to teach them to respect my wife," he threatened.

Miriam, knowing he was a man of action when aroused, tried to soothe him. "Superstition is not easily overcome. It takes time."

That year winter arrived early. Day after day the overcast sky sent down a fresh layer of snow, and the biting winds kept piling it higher and higher at the doorsteps of the houses. The people shivered and complained that this was the bitterest winter within memory. They grumbled that their wood supply was not enough to keep them warm. Not that there wasn't plenty of wood in the forest, but each family was allowed to cut only a certain amount. They were well aware that the town council, wishing to preserve and not despoil the forest, was keeping a watchful eye on the woodcutters.

Some of the people were certain that such miserable weather could only be the work of an evil spirit. Among themselves they accused Miriam. "This witch, she is responsible for it."

Spring at last arrived. The warm sun, melting away the snow, brought cheer to the winter-weary people of Shawshine. The stream overflowed, and the countryside had never been so green as it was that summer.

And then winter was at their door again. Remembering the trials of the past winter, the people took good care to stock their woodpiles as high as they were permitted. But days passed, one more balmy than the last, and hardly a flake of snow came down from the sky during the entire winter. There was no snow for the spring sun to melt, and the summer heat that followed threatened to dry up whatever water there was in the stream. The sun beat down from a cloudless sky, scorching the pastures. There was hardly any feed or water for the cattle. As the stream became too shallow for traveling, the farmers had no way of bringing their corn to the mill and Benjamin was forced to close down.

The people were in despair. This was the worst drought they had suffered in a long time. Gathering at the meetinghouse, they prayed, "Please, Lord, let the bottles of heaven be unstopped."

As the drought continued, their wrath once more turned against Miriam Fay. "We never had all this trouble until that woman came to live here," they muttered. Even when the rains finally came and the countryside reclaimed its normal richness, this suspicion still remained with them.

Years went by, and Benjamin Fay was now the father of three beautiful black-eyed children. "The spit'n' image of their mother," he would say proudly. It was precisely this resemblance that made the parents in town warn their children as they left for school, "Mind, stay away from the Fay children."

It was the custom among the townspeople to take turns giving board to their schoolmaster throughout the year as part payment for his service. When Miriam's turn came, she was very generous. But even the schoolmaster's recounting of her exceptional kindness didn't persuade the people to forget their prejudice against her and her black-eyed children.

Suddenly a mysterious plague attacking children swept the town. None of the townspeople, not even the minister, had any notion of how to cope with it. Mournfully they saw one after another of their children sicken and die. However, they didn't fail to notice that the Fay children remained untouched by the dreadful disease. "Few people ever come near Fay's home; that must be the reason," a kind person tried to explain, but no one wanted to hear such a reasonable explanation.

Meanwhile Miriam was busily brewing a concoction of tansy in her fireplace. Trying it on her children, she found it helped prevent them from catching the disease. Cheered and eager to help other children, she threw on her mantle and hurried off to town, knocking on doors and offering her remedy. The townspeople, seeing Miriam in her dreaded scarlet mantle, at first wanted none of her aid. However, becoming frantic as the disease raged on, they finally agreed to let her attend their children.

Miriam worked tirelessly, and when the disease was at last arrested, people reluctantly had to admit that it was possible for a witch to do one good deed along with so many evil ones.

Years passed, and the country became caught up in the fight for independence. The people of Shawshine were tense, never knowing when the redcoats would descend upon them. They were constantly on the watch for traitors, and a single wrong word sometimes was sufficient to brand a person as a Tory.

One day, hearing about a gathering at the meetinghouse for the purpose of raising money for the regiment training outside the town, Miriam hurried there. She no longer wore her scarlet mantle, which was made of English cloth. In fact, she was the first one in town to refuse to use the tea so outrageously overtaxed

by the British, and everything else exported by the hated oppressors.

"What can I do to help?" she asked the gathering. She waited expectantly. Meeting with silence and suspicious glances, she responded with a mysterious smile and walked out.

Shortly after that meeting she was seen in the early mornings wearing her scarlet mantle and perched on the miller's horse, galloping back home from somewhere. What was she up to? the townspeople demanded. There was no doubt left in their minds — Miriam Fay was a spy working for the enemy.

The officers in the enemy camp were glad to see a native woman wearing the color of their red coats and also friendly to them. "What can you do for us?" they asked one evening when she entered their camp.

"Those Yankees are stubborn fighters, you know," she replied evasively.

"So they are," the commanding officer grumbled. "Do you have any useful information for us?"

"For a proper reward maybe I have," she said cunningly. After the reward money was agreed upon, she told them of a tunnel where a storehouse full of ammunition and foodstuff was hidden. She would lead them there herself.

Late the following night she secretly met the

group of officers at a prearranged spot near a stream where a wooden plank thrown across served as a bridge. Instructing the officers to leave their horses with the moneybags tied to the saddles at the stream, she led them on foot across the makeshift bridge and into a nearby cavern.

When they were well within the cavern, suddenly the light of Miriam's lantern went out and pitch-darkness descended. "Ho, what happened?" the officers shouted, but no reply came from the woman in the scarlet mantle.

In the enveloping darkness Miriam stole swiftly out of the cavern and, after crossing the plank, threw it down into the stream. Snatching the moneybags and slapping the horses, sending them galloping in different directions, she hurried back to town.

The sun had moved up high in the sky when the weary British officers finally managed to get back to their camp. They sheepishly told their commanding officer what had happened.

"We were outwitted by a woman deceitfully wearing a mantle the color of our uniforms. Best that we never mention this shameful affair to anyone," he cautioned.

Miriam wasted no time in confronting the townspeople and triumphantly handing over the moneybags filled with golden crowns. Amazed and then delighted, they listened to the tale of her secret mission. "Thank heaven!" they exclaimed. "Now we can outfit our fighters with everything they need." Completely forgotten was Miriam the so-called witch; instead she was now Miriam the brave patriot and the woman of fine virtue.

The town Cochichawick, eventually renamed Andover, and Shawshine, now called Bedford, still remember Miriam Fay, one of the most courageous women of the American Revolution.

The Riddle of the Room Upstairs

Hunched on his horse, young Tom Drake, a native of Massachusetts, was plodding on a lonely path heading north. He was sorry for himself. Coward, the villagers had branded him. He didn't mind being called names when he refused to risk his life by joining others in a chase after dangerous horse thieves. But when he was called a Tory because he didn't volunteer to join the army fighting the English, staying in the village became unbearable. He was neither a coward nor a Tory, but he did not choose to fight.

The sky was becoming increasingly threatening, and the whipping wind made it difficult for his horse to make much headway. Straining his eyes, he tried to detect a human dwelling where he could stop for the night, but all he could see was endless stretches of wild country. As darkness was setting in, he thought wearily, "I guess the only thing left for me is to spend the night under a tree."

Nevertheless he rode on. The path now led up a hill that was covered with brush and scattered stubby trees. Suddenly he pulled at the reins. "God be praised," he exclaimed, almost jumping out of his saddle. "There is a village down there! Come on, Browny, get going!" he said as he kicked the horse with his spurs.

His cheerfulness increased as he approached the village. Not only was it large, but it even had an inn. There were tall trees in front of the inn with troughs for horses beneath them.

Before dismounting, Tom Drake took a good look at the inn. It was an old rambling building with a long two-story shed attached. The upper floor of the shed was unfinished, and the openings left for windows were loosely boarded up. Below were stalls for the carriages of traveling guests. "It certainly is a popular tavern," he thought, noticing that the stalls were well-filled. "Will there be room for me?"

Innkeeper Marshall, wearing a long white apron over his portly figure, stepped forward to greet Tom as he entered the low-ceilinged room of the tavern. Hearing that he wanted lodging for the night, the innkeeper spread his hands regretfully. "Sorry, my good man, but all my rooms are filled. Unless..." For a few moments the innkeeper regarded Tom silently, then said, "I do have a room, but it has been empty for a long time. It's — well, it's haunted. Of course I wouldn't think of offering it to you."

"A haunted room is all you have?" Tom exclaimed. His immediate impulse was to reject it. Then reminded of his reputation as a coward, he braced himself and said, "Do I look like a man who would be afraid of ghosts? I'll sleep in that room."

The innkeeper hesitated. He had tried various means to rid that room of ghosts but had failed. Perhaps this courageous man would stand up against them and discourage them from ever returning. "Very well," he said. "But remember that I warned you." Handing Tom a lamp and a warming pan, he led him up the stairs, pointed to a room along the hall, and hurriedly retreated.

Tiptoeing to the door, Tom put an ear to it and, hearing nothing, touched the handle. The door opened with a creak, but no other sounds came from inside the room. Entering, he looked around and was relieved to find that it was very much like the rooms he had seen in taverns back home. There was the same kind of low-beamed ceiling, a wide wooden bed, and a washstand with a bowl and pitcher for water. He felt the bed with his hand and, satisfied, tumbled into it and at once fell asleep.

He didn't know how long he slept, but suddenly he sat up fully awake. He had a peculiar sensation that someone had been touching him and tickling his toes. "There must be a ghost amusing himself at my expense," he thought, and looked around half expecting to find something lurking in a corner.

As the kerosene in the lamp was running low, its light was flickering uncertainly, causing long shadows in the room to move and change their shapes as though they were alive. "There's really nothing in this room to be scared of," Tom tried to reassure himself. He was about to go back to sleep when he saw little dark shapes sneaking in from under the crack of the door, whirling about the room, and vanishing through the crack again. "If you are the imps of Satan, in the name of God declare yourselves!" he shouted.

The dark creatures, evidently heeding his warning, stopped scurrying about the room. After waiting awhile, he decided to try to sleep again. "I must prove I am not a coward," he reminded himself, but nevertheless threw the quilt over his head.

A muffled noise, then a loud gruesome groan made him throw off the quilt and listen. The groan went on, becoming louder, then weaker, then louder again. Frightened, he scanned the room, trying to detect someone or something that was causing it. Seeing nothing, he waited.

In the midst of the groaning and moaning he could now distinctly hear sounds of a strange instrument, accompanied by metallic clanking. "Satan or ghost, show your face!" he cried. But the only reply he received was a chorus of groans and renewed clanging. Terrified, he jumped out of bed and, without pausing to give himself an account of what he was doing, ran out of the room.

Downstairs the quiet of the tavern was reassuring. The fireplace, though the fire had died down, was still giving off warmth. Tom sank into a chair nearby and soon fell asleep.

The rays of dawn were peering into the tavern when Tom Drake opened his eyes to find the innkeeper standing over him.

"You're an early riser," the innkeeper greeted him. "Did you sleep well in that room?"

"Slept as fast as a baby in the cradle," Tom replied casually.

"And you were not disturbed and didn't see anything?"

"There was nothing to be disturbed by," Tom

asserted. "I hope your breakfast will be as good as the room."

The innkeeper regarded him with pleasure. "You're a brave man," he said. "I trust you've discouraged the spirits from ever coming back to that room." To show his appreciation, he treated Tom to an especially fine breakfast.

But Tom Drake was hardly in the mood to enjoy his food. Breakfasting hurriedly, he left, vowing to himself never to come near the cursed tavern again.

The next few nights not many travelers came by asking for lodging, and the room where Tom Drake had slept remained unused. That was until Samuel Holt, a prosperous wine merchant, drove up in his two-horse carriage. After exchanging greetings with the innkeeper, who came out to meet him, he declared, "I'm in need of a good night's rest, my friend. Make the room ready for me, the one I had three months ago."

"Ah, the room you had is not available tonight," the innkeeper said lightly. "But I have a room which hasn't been in use for a while that is every bit as nice as the other."

As there was nothing else he could do, the merchant accepted the offer. "At least I'm not too late for supper, I hope," he grumbled.

The wine merchant had a healthy appetite as well as a big capacity for food, and the ritual of being served and eating extended into the late hours of the evening. At last with a satisfied yawn the merchant declared it was time for him to retire. "Take me to that confounded room," he demanded.

Lighting a lamp for his guest, the innkeeper readily showed him the way upstairs. "A good and peaceful night to you," he offered before parting.

The innkeeper was still cleaning up with his helpers after the evening meal when the merchant came running downstairs in his nightshirt and cap, carrying his clothes. "What kind of a room did you give me? It's haunted!" he bellowed. It was some time before he could compose himself enough to tell about the weird noises, groans, and clankings he heard.

The innkeeper listened, shaking his head. "So the spirits came back," he said mournfully. To pacify the panic-stricken merchant, he offered him his own bed, while he proposed to make the best of it by sleeping on the floor at the fireplace.

The merchant had his carriage readied early the following morning and departed complaining loudly about the miserable night he had spent in the inn.

The unhappy innkeeper spent the morning brooding over the return of the evil spirits to that room, fearing it would be a threat to the reputation of his inn. "What can I do to get rid of them forever?" he wondered. He finally decided to seek advice from the wise men in the village.

"There once was a haunted house nearby. The house burnt down to the ground, and well that it did," one of the men recalled.

"Quite possibly those are the very spirits who now are lodging in your inn," another man suggested.

For a while the men were silent, thinking it over. Suddenly one of them had an idea. "I hear that a magician is now traveling in our part of the country," he said to the innkeeper. "Perhaps you could induce him to come and try his magic power."

Everybody, including the innkeeper, decided this was an excellent idea. The magician was soon located and persuaded to come to the inn.

Potter, a short stocky man with a big head, bushy hair, and piercing eyes, was an experienced magician. However, traveling as he did from village to village with his bag of tricks, he barely managed to make enough money to pay for his daily needs. Now, miracle of miracles, he was offered room and board in an inn — and free!

"I've heard about your great skill as a magi-

cian," the innkeeper said. "There is a room upstairs which is ruining the reputation of my inn.
It is haunted by strange spirits. Perhaps you,
with your magical powers, could drive them
away?"

Potter took time to reply. There was no way of
knowing whether he could perform such a difficult task. "It will be a challenge," he finally
declared. "I will sleep in that room tonight."

The night was starless, and the swirling wind
blew chilling air into the house through all the
cracks and crannies. Potter stayed at the fireplace until the logs burned down. At last, bidding the waiting innkeeper good night, he
climbed the stairs.

As he opened the door of the haunted room, a
swarm of dark little creatures scurried under the
bed. He drew back startled. What could they
be? He didn't get into bed, but sat up keeping
the lamp ready at his side, alert for any further
movement or sound. Suddenly he heard a groan
coming from right outside the room. For a while
the groan went on, but no sooner did it subside
when wheezy moans and clanking sounds
started up.

Potter the magician, who lived in a world of
tricks, decided he must find the cause of those
weird sounds. Listening intently, he noticed
that when the wind outside the inn increased,

the groan became louder. Determined to track down its source, he tapped the walls of the room until he discovered a hidden door. Prying it ajar, he found that it opened out into the shed. As he stepped forward, guided by the light of his lamp, hundreds of pigeons roosting there stirred. Mice scuttled between his feet, and bats flew over his head. As the bats swooped down, their wings brushed against the chain strung across a partly boarded-up window, making it vibrate with the clanking noise he had heard.

Smiling at this discovery, the magician started to look for other clues. A gust of wind tore into the loft, its force making the old rafters creak and groan. "Quite a simple explanation after all!" he thought.

Encouraged, he continued his search. Moving his lamp in all directions, he noticed a sick pigeon lying not far off. Every breath it drew ended in a wheeze and a moan. "Good Lord, the poor thing is suffering from asthma!" the magician exclaimed. Feeling sorry for the bird, he put the lamp down to pick up the pigeon. His attention was caught by a large swaying splinter of wood. As he watched, a gust of wind banged the splinter against a nail that had been driven in close to it. "So this is what produced the musical sounds!"

Wasting no more time, he removed the chain

and the splinter and carefully tucked the asthmatic pigeon into a bag, planning to set it free again a good distance away from the inn. This done, he returned to his room and contentedly went to sleep.

In the morning he told the innkeeper, "I got rid of the ghosts. I promise they will never disturb you again."

"Bless you!" the innkeeper said. "How ever did you do it?"

"By using all my magical powers," Potter replied mysteriously.

Before long, Potter's amazing feat became known throughout the colony. Wherever he went he found that most people admired him for it. But there were some, including Tom Drake who had actually experienced the ghostly noises, who feared the magician might be in league with the Devil.

Dancing Stones

There were many reasons George Walton disapproved of his neighbor. When her temper was aroused, she was as uncontrollable as a wild horse, sputtering words no decent person would use. When walking alone on the road, she would mutter to someone visible only to her. It was some years since this woman and her husband had come to settle in Portsmouth and build their home next to his. He didn't mind them, for they seemed to be as hardworking folk as any in that part of New Hampshire. But after her husband died, the woman was never the same, behaving as queerly as though guided by the Devil himself.

Early one bright spring morning, George Walton decided to make the rounds of his land. As he trod on the damp ground, thinking of all the hard labor it had taken to clear it, he saw his neighbor busily working in the field. With her back bent, her hair disheveled, she looked like an old crooked wind-blown tree.

A sudden thought seized George Walton. Although his boundaries had never been clearly defined, that strip of land the woman was working was really his! Waving his hands indignantly, he came running toward her.

"What seems to be the trouble, neighbor?" she asked, straightening up.

"This strip of land is mine. You have no right to work it!" he shouted.

"Don't you shout at me, you shameless crow," she retorted. "My husband and I cleared this strip and have been working it ever since we first settled here, and I mean to go on doing so."

"Get off my land or I'll make the court order you off," George Walton persisted.

"Go to the Devil if that pleases you," she growled, bending down as if to pick up a stone. Seeing him hurrying away, she shouted after him. "Should you rob me of this land, you'll never peacefully enjoy it!"

The woman's threat made George Walton jittery, for it crossed his mind that she might have the power of witchcraft. But when he looked up at his spacious two-storied house with its steep sloping roof in the front, he was reassured. Being a prosperous and respected planter, he should have no difficulty getting the court to confirm his claim.

George Walton was not mistaken; shortly afterward the court did grant him the right to that strip of land.

One Sunday night Walton, his wife, and their four children were sleeping peacefully when violent crashes suddenly rattled the whole house, making them jump out of their beds in panic. It seemed as if cannonballs were being hurled on the roof and against the sides of the house.

"Could it be a summer hailstorm?" Walton's wife cried.

"Nonsense," Walton replied, trying to keep calm in spite of the deafening bombardment.

The moment the crashes stopped, the Waltons hurried out to see what might be causing this awful attack. There was not a cloud in the sky and the moon was shining peacefully. They saw absolutely no one.

"I just heard a rustle among the trees!" one of the children exclaimed.

Walton strained his ears, but hearing nothing, shook his head scornfully. "Now don't start imagining things," he said. Nevertheless he went on looking around to make sure no one was hiding nearby. Then he noticed that his fence had been torn off its hinges and flung into a field some distance away.

"Could have been a strong gust of wind that caused this," he said uncertainly. "Anyway, we'll find out more in the morning."

As they were about to go back into the house, a shower of rocks came down all around them. They scuttled for the porch, glad that they had miraculously escaped being hit.

"Get into the house!" Walton shouted, as a new volley of rocks came flying onto the porch. Making sure that all of his family was accounted for, he locked and bolted the doors and the windows. But although the rock throwing stopped, the family still remained wary and ill at ease.

"No need sitting up; go to bed, all of you," Walton told them after a while.

"I'll wager there'll be more rocks coming," one of the boys declared.

As if that were a signal, the bombardment started again with even more fury than before. Some stones came smashing through the window, landing in the room. Some came hurtling down the chimney, bouncing and rebounding like balls. All the terror-stricken family could do was watch the flying stones and try to keep out of their way. It was two hours before the onslaught finally stopped and they could get some sleep.

Although nothing unusual happened during the following day, George Walton went on brooding over the frightful scare of the previous night. And when after supper the family went to bed, he remained awake, pacing the floor of his room, trying to puzzle out the cause of the stone throwing. "A silly mischief, not worth bothering about," he finally decided. He had just started getting undressed when a hammer came down from the ceiling, making a deep dent in the floor right at his feet and narrowly missing him. "How could this happen?" he cried out. As he raised his eyes to the ceiling, the candles were swept off the table, leaving him in complete darkness. Too bewildered to try to find the candles, Walton flopped on his bed, expecting more things to happen, until at last sleep overtook him.

For the next four or five days the Walton family were left undisturbed. Then one day as they were finishing their dinner, the stone throwing started again. To find out whether the stones bouncing back and forth were the same ones, Walton marked some and put them on the table in a row. At that moment there was a knock at the door. "Strange," he thought, "The door was left open; there's no need to knock." Nevertheless he went to the door, but found no one there.

"Look, Father — the stones you put on the table are flying around again!" one of the boys called to him.

Walton turned around and watched the marked stones bouncing about the room. "Must be an invisible spirit playing these devilish tricks," he said, completely puzzled.

As if in reply, a piece of brick from the fireplace tumbled out and landed on the floor, and the iron spit flew up the chimney, then came down again. When a stone came rolling toward Walton, he picked it up to see if it was one of those he had marked. He found it so hot that he immediately dropped it.

By the time all this commotion subsided, Walton was completely exhausted and as nervous as a hounded fox. Would these evil tricks ever end, he wondered? It occurred to him that he hadn't seen his neighbor for some time. But when he looked out of the window, there she was, poking around outside her house calmly as if she had nothing whatsoever to do with the disturbance.

Tired as he was after a poorly spent night, George Walton went out the following morning to do his usual day's work in the field. Absorbed in his work, he almost forgot the horrors he had gone through.

All of a sudden his horses began to pull back and forth, kicking the ground with their hoofs and snorting wildly. Some of his workmen hurried over and tried to help quiet the horses, but it was useless, for the frightened animals went on acting as though they were possessed.

"The witch is at it again," Walton muttered, looking around to see if his neighbor was lurking somewhere nearby. "Watch out!" he shouted to his wife and youngest child walking toward him, as a hail of stones came pouring over the field. However, his warning was unnecessary, for the mysterious barrage stopped as suddenly as it began. Just as weird was the behavior of his horses, now standing meekly as though nothing had ever disturbed them.

Could it be your boys, playing tricks to amuse themselves?" one of Walton's helpers asked. At that very moment a stone hit Walton's child in the back so painfully that Mrs. Walton had to carry him home quickly.

In spite of all this, George Walton stayed on in the field till the sun went down. On the way to his house, remembering the shattered windows, he thought he might take a look at what repairs they would require. What he saw on entering his backyard was an unbelievable sight. Some of the bales of hay he had stored up to feed his animals were hanging down from the trees. Other bales had been torn apart, and the hay twisted into all sorts of shapes and stuck up all over the back of the house as though some fantastic festival were about to take place.

Walton stared at the fiendish display with clenched fists, but he appeared calm when he came into the house, and said nothing at the supper table. They were half finished with their meal when Mrs. Walton suddenly sat up looking as pale as a ghost. "There is a hand at the window! A hand without a body!" she cried out.

"Maybe the Devil wants to have supper with us," the older boy offered.

Walton gave him an angry look and went out to the porch to see. As he expected, he found no trace of anyone there. "Can't we even have our supper in peace?" he grumbled.

There was no stone throwing that evening, and Walton was thankful that he and his family were able to spend the night undisturbed.

Hearing of Walton's distress, some of his neighbors came to see if they could be of any help. One of them, to distract him, brought his recorder, offering to play this flutelike instrument for him.

"I believe the worst is over," Walton assured him. "Just the same, it would be nice to hear some music."

His friend readily obliged. He was a skillful player and was often called onto perform. He started slowly but as he played on he picked up vigor, and soon the tune came forth with whirling speed. That proved to be a mistake. As if unable to resist the temptation, stones came rolling into the room and, forming a circle, began swaying and jumping to his tune. The people gasped, and their astonishment became even greater when a pewter spoon came gliding out and joined the dancing circle. After the music stopped and the stones, accompanied by the spoon, bounced out through the open door, it took the neighbors quite a while to regain their speech.

"Nobody could make me believe this if I hadn't seen it myself!" one of the women guests declared, shaking her head.

Agreeing with her, each one wisely offered a remedy for getting rid of the evil spirit. They set about to make a brew to ward off a possible further attack.

At first this remedy didn't help, as the terrible stone throwing went on for several more weeks. Then abruptly it stopped and never returned. However, the talk and concern about

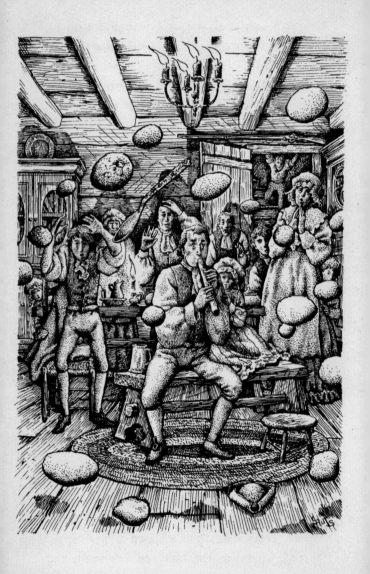

George Walton's mysterious persecution continued for a long time afterward. There were only a few who believed that it was really the work of some youthful mischief makers. But there were many who insisted that no human being could play such tricks. Nothing could shake their belief that only the Devil and his witches had the power and the will to make stones come alive. Of course, George Walton was sure he knew who one of the witches was — his neighbor.

The Witch Who Spoke
in Many Tongues

It did not take long for the villagers of New Haven, Connecticut, to brand Ann Jones a witch. They could understand that coming from the Dutch settlement, New Amsterdam, she would speak Dutch as well as English. But when they heard her spouting strange sounds unlike any language they knew, that was too much for them. Also disquieting was the rumor that she possessed the power of communicating with animals.

Everything about Ann Jones radiated youth — her movements, graceful as a doe, her lovely dark eyes, and a complexion glowing with health. Nevertheless, the villagers were not deceived by the girl's appearance. "Her youthful face is but a mask," they asserted. "Someday we'll snatch off that mask and expose her true face, that of a decrepit wrinkled witch."

Nor were her parents able to gain the trust of the villagers. The spacious house her father built with its slanting roof and a gable on each end didn't help either. It was far too costly and showy to suit the simple taste of the villagers. Squatter, they called him contemptuously, though they knew full well he had paid a handsome price for his land.

One day two village women, passing by the Jones's backyard, heard a sheep baa and another sheep answering. "Strange," the older woman said, puzzled. "I am quite sure those Joneses have only one sheep."

Peering over the fence, the other woman said, "That's right, and I see only one there. Ah, there's Ann in the yard. Why, she's the one talking to the sheep!"

For a while the two women stood staring speechlessly into the yard. "We might do well to report this to the Justice of Peace," the older woman whispered. "She's a witch."

Her companion considered a moment and shook her head. "We couldn't prove she's causing any harm. But she'll be caught someday just as sure as a man can catch a lame rabbit."

The sight of Mrs. Jones stepping out of the

house and wearing a mountain of petticoats momentarily made them forget about Ann.

"Look at her, piling up more than a dozen petticoats on herself and not being ashamed of it," the older woman grumbled.

"It's sinful to wear them that short," the other one agreed. "Her ankles are plain for anyone to see."

"She's doing it on purpose, to show her boots and buckles. You can see they're made of pure silver. Some pair, mother and daughter," the older woman snorted, and motioned to her companion to move on.

Although the villagers had little doubt that Ann had supernatural powers, as long as she was harmless, they left her alone. But then they noticed that Robert Hall, usually a steady and hardworking young man, was behaving strangely. Completely bewitched by that girl's charms, he was following her around like a puppy and staying up nights at her window. That was dismaying enough, but when other young men began to show signs of the same affliction, the villagers were aroused to action.

Accused of using her witchcraft on innocent young people, Ann was arrested and brought before the judge. Cries arose from the gathering in the courtroom, "She is a witch, a dangerous witch! Let her rot in prison!"

Witnesses were called to testify, but Hall and the other young men thought to be afflicted refused to admit that they were under a witch's spell. Without their cooperation the unhappy judge could do nothing but warn the girl not to use her evil charms in the future and let her go free.

As Ann was walking out from the courthouse, she was approached by Mrs. Eyers, a middle-aged woman much respected by the villagers.

"I've heard so much about your talents," Mrs. Eyers said amiably. "Come with me to my house; I wish to converse with you."

Ann readily agreed, and from that day on she was seen visiting Mrs. Eyers quite often. "She's woven her spell around poor Mrs. Eyers," some of the neighbors whispered.

Nothing escaped the watchful eyes of the villagers. They saw Ann taking walks in the country, and neither pouring rain nor blizzard seemed to bother her. She would climb steep rocks and jump over them as though she were playing tag with an invisible spirit.

Bizarre things were surely happening. Someone claimed he came upon Ann riding on a broomstick. Someone else positively saw her soaring over brooms and horseshoes lying on the ground as though she were lifted on invisible wings, all the while humming rhyming words.

But the most astonishing tale was told by one old villager. Driving his cow home from pasture late one afternoon, he suddenly stopped short. There was the girl walking, and she wasn't alone! With her was a creature limping on what was obviously a cloven foot. It could be none other than the Devil himself, and she holding onto his arm as though she were married to him!

These tales started people worrying even more about Mrs. Eyers, since she was permitting Ann to be so constant a visitor. Some tried to advise her to stop seeing the girl. When this failed, they asked their minister to warn her of the danger of being won over by a witch. "I've heard about these visits," the minister said calmly. "But I know Mrs. Eyers is a good honest woman with a strong character. She can be trusted. Just the same, I shall keep an eye on her."

One day a woman passing by Mrs. Eyers's house was unable to resist peeping into an open kitchen window. It was not the first time she had done so, for she knew of no other kitchen so well-equipped. There was the big fireplace with its fine assortment of cooking pots; shining pewter plates neatly arranged on sideboards; rows of saucepans, dippers, and all sorts of utensils hanging down from shelves; and brass warming pans and fancy platters adorning the paneled walls.

Dazzled by the glittering array, she did not at first notice the two figures sitting in a corner of the kitchen. "That's Ann and the Devil talking together!" she gasped, and hurried off to sound the alarm in the village.

Mrs. Eyers happened to be visiting a friend at the other end of the village when she heard about what was discovered in her kitchen. She rushed to her house, only to find it already surrounded by a mob arguing over the best means of capturing the evil pair trapped inside.

"Imagine, if we could bring the Devil in person before the Justice of Peace, our village would be the first to accomplish such a miraculous feat!"

Taking charge, Mrs. Eyers ordered, "Close all the shutters!" When this was done, she made the crowd help her stop up all the holes and cracks of the house. Then she told the people to guard it from all sides and keep a careful eye on the chimney on the roof in case the Devil might try to escape from there.

"What are we waiting for! Break into the house and grab them!" the crowd demanded.

However, Mrs. Eyers wouldn't be rushed. Choosing a few from among the crowd, she motioned them to follow her. Stealthily opening the door to the kitchen, she squeezed herself inside, the others close behind her. Quickly they

lit the lamp and were amazed to find no one in the room. They looked in every corner, in all the closets; they searched the cellar and looked up the chimney, but discovered no trace of either Ann or the Devil. There was nothing for the searchers left to do but come out and tell the waiting crowd the disappointing news.

"How could they have escaped?" the crowd asked the minister, standing in their midst.

"Who knows all the Devil's tricks?" the minister replied gravely. Then with an unexpected twinkle in his eye, he added, "Perhaps the evil spirits of the girl and the Devil entered into two men of the searching party and flew out as the men left the house."

Never again was Ann seen in the village of New Haven. Shortly after the girl disappeared, her mother also left the village. "Good riddance!" people said. "Who cares to have a mother of such a cursed daughter in our midst?" Ann's friend Hall too moved away, explaining that he wanted to go north to make a new life for himself. Of course the villagers went on talking about the girl, claiming that the Devil must have taken her for himself. Except Mrs. Eyers, who carefully avoided even mentioning the girl's name again.

It happened that some years later the minister of New Haven asked a friend going to Vermont to try to locate a family there by the name of Hall. Finding Hall's house, the traveler knocked at the door and was taken aback when a fine-looking woman came out smiling at him as though glad to see an old friend.

"If you are Mrs. Hall, I have a letter for you from the minister of New Haven," the traveler said.

Still smiling, the woman took the letter and said, "Don't you recognize me?"

"Yes, I thought you looked vaguely familiar," the traveler replied. "Now, where was it I met you?"

"In New Haven, I'm sure," the woman said laughing. "I'm Ann Jones, the one the villagers believed was a witch." She invited him into the house and told him how it happened that she was now living in Vermont. She had had to flee for her life from New Haven because she was branded as a sorceress. The villagers believed that she had bewitched Hall, who had taken a liking to her. And when the villagers discovered that she spoke a strange tongue, they became even more suspicious of her. They had no way of knowing that it was a gentleman living in a cave on West Rock who had taught her the mysterious language, which was really Latin.

"I didn't know someone was living in the cave," the traveler said.

"It was a well-kept secret. Only the minister, Mrs. Eyers, and I knew about his hiding place. My job was to take food to him. In exchange, he taught me Latin and many things about the world and people. Occasionally he would steal away from the cave and stay in Mrs. Eyers's house."

"I am still puzzled about how you managed to escape from her house while it was so closely surrounded and thoroughly searched," the traveler said.

It was quite simple, Ann told him. There was a closet hidden behind a panel in the kitchen. So well did it blend with the other panels, and so cleverly was it covered by kitchen utensils, that no one would suspect a secret closet there. She and the fugitive were talking in the kitchen when Mrs. Eyers closed the window shutters, thus signaling them that they had to hide. She remained in hiding in her friend's house until her future husband was able to meet her outside the village. After long traveling they settled here. She still corresponded with Mrs. Eyers.

"Who exactly was that fugitive you so respected. Or is it still a secret?" the traveler asked.

"No, there is no longer the need to keep it secret, for the man is dead now," Ann replied. "He was William Goffe, one of the judges responsible for the beheading of the English King, Charles I."

She went on to explain as long as Cromwell, who succeeded the beheaded Charles I, was in power the judge was safe. After Cromwell died and the monarchy was restored, William Goffe had fled from England and come to America. Soon after his arrival the colonies came under the rule of the new English king, and the poor man had to spend the rest of his life in hiding.

"He was truly a remarkable man," Ann concluded.

The traveler smiled and said, "And you are a remarkable woman, so unjustly branded the witch of many tongues."

The Seafaring Wizard

The schooner Neptune was plowing through the choppy waters of the Atlantic on the way home from a long voyage to the West Indies. A threatening black cloud was moving over the sky and the increasing wind tore at the sails, tossing the ship about. In spite of the danger of being swept off the deck, the sailors worked frantically to keep the ship at even keel.

"Look!" one of the sailors suddenly shouted, pointing into the depth of the water between two high waves.

Holding on to their ropes, the others stared into the sea. "A sea serpent! It must be at least fifty feet long!" they cried.

The young sailor Caleb Powell, who was working across the deck, came rushing over demanding, "What's the excitement about?"

"A sea serpent swimming in a circle. Ah, it just disappeared!"

"Nonsense," Caleb Powell said with a shrug. "Must be a dolphin."

Disregarding him, the sailors went on talking excitedly about the fantastic dark monster that for a time seemed to be following their ship. Some of them were now positive it was a hundred feet long, with eight sections each the size of an enormous barrel and a protruding tongue that was at least three feet long and shaped like a harpoon. They kept assuring each other that they were lucky the monster had not attacked the ship, and hoped they had seen the last of it.

By evening, as the ship was nearing their home port of Newburyport, Massachusetts, the wind had subsided, and the moon appeared through the broken clouds. The schooner regained its bearing on the calmer sea and proudly sailed on. The sailors, forgetting their fright, turned their minds to the pleasures awaiting them ashore.

While resting, Powell and a companion were exchanging tales of their adventures in the West Indies when another sailor came hurriedly down the rigging, almost losing his balance. "A hand sticking out of the water, over there!" he cried, motioning in the direction of the horizon.

The three sailors gazed with awe at a dark shape, silhouetted against the evening sky, that did look like an enormous hand emerging from the sea. Ominous and terrifying, it lingered there for a while, then gradually faded and vanished.

"The hand of Satan," Powell's companion declared.

"Maybe," Powell allowed. Then he added soberly, "Maybe it was just a cloud the shape of a hand."

For a few moments both sailors regarded him incredulously. "Say," his friend burst out indignantly. "Are you denying what you saw with your own eyes? Or are you one of those who don't believe there are such things as evil spirits or demons?" Making a violent gesture, he moved away without waiting for an answer.

For the remainder of the voyage Powell's shipmate ignored him, and after the ship docked at Newburyport he walked off his separate way without so much as a parting word.

When not at sea, Caleb Powell stayed in the small clapboard house that had belonged to his parents. He didn't have many friends in the town. "Visiting foreign lands made him too smart for his own good," the townspeople complained. Among the few people Caleb did go to see occasionally was the cobbler William Morse, who with his wife and their eleven-year-old grandson John Stiles lived across the street from him.

William Morse was working at the cobbler's bench in his house with the front door open when he saw Caleb trudging along the road, his sailor's bag on his shoulder. "Welcome home, sailor!" Morse called, beckoning him. As Caleb stopped at his door, he said, "Come in, sit you down and tell me about your journey."

Caleb picked up a stool and was about to place it near the cobbler's bench when a shoe came flying across the room, just missing Morse.

"What's that?" Caleb asked.

"Nothing, nothing," the cobbler replied, nervously looking around. "I'm used to that."

"Obviously that old shoe doesn't like the idea of being repaired," Caleb said, laughing. As if challenging him, another old shoe came flying across the room, this time crashing against the wall. Caleb started to rush out to try to catch the mischief-maker, but the cobbler stopped him.

"No use looking; you won't find anyone," he said.

"How long has this been going on?"

The house was bewitched, Morse told Caleb. Besides shoes flying about the room, there were other strange things happening. One time his tools would disappear while he was working at the bench; another time brickbats and pieces of shoe leather would be hurled down the chimney. This had been going on for some time. "My only hope is that the evil spirit causing all this will eventually get tired and leave me in peace," he concluded.

They sat in silence, waiting. After a while, as nothing more happened, Morse urged, "Now tell me about your adventures."

"We had pretty rough sailing, but it was worth it," Caleb told him.

As he was relating the wonders of the West Indies, the back door opened a crack and a boy's freckled face appeared. "Ho, John!" Caleb called to him. Caught listening, the boy entered the room belligerently, as if daring anyone to throw him out. He was a stocky fellow, with restless little eyes and a flock of red hair badly in need of a good brushing. His clothes too could have stood some mending, as well as his shoes where his toes showed through.

"Have you finished cleaning up the back-yard?" his grandfather wanted to know.

"Almost," John squeezed through his teeth.

"Then go and finish it. And don't forget to feed the pig."

"Oh, all right," the boy grumbled. Turning his freckled face to Caleb, he asked, "In those lands you've been talking about, does food really grow on trees and you don't have to work to get it?"

"Not quite," Caleb replied, laughing. "But I did see boys climbing trees just like monkeys and helping themselves to all the coconuts and bananas they wanted."

The boy shuffled his feet, thinking it over, then without saying anything left the room. Caleb then remembered that he hadn't been home himself yet. "Good to see you, neighbor," he said, picking up his sailor's bag.

The following day Caleb Powell went to visit his ailing brother in Gloucester. On returning a week later he found the cobbler in a desperate mood.

"There is no peace in my house. The evil spirit won't leave me alone," he lamented "I can't work — I don't know what to do."

Sorry as Caleb was for his neighbor's plight, he could think of no way to help him.

But it happened one rainy morning that Caleb, passing the cobbler's house, decided to peer into the window to see how his neighbor was doing. He found Morse and his wife on their knees praying together. As he watched them, wondering if their prayers would really discourage the evil spirit, a shoe came flying into the room and bounced against the ceiling. Quickly glancing in the direction it had come from, he saw the boy hiding under an armchair. So the evil spirit was the little rascal! Caleb couldn't help laughing, and knocked on the door.

"Still troubled by the evil spirit?" he asked the cobbler. Getting only a dejected nod in reply, Caleb went on, "I've been thinking about it. I believe I have the power to help you, provided you let me take John for the day."

Morse shook his head doubtfully. "How would that help?" Then, thinking it over, he said, "Go ahead, take him. I'm willing to try anything."

At first the boy stubbornly refused to go with the sailor. "I know, you want me to do some work around your house," he grumbled. When he was told he wouldn't have to do any chores at all, he still refused. It was only when Caleb promised to tell him more about the sea and the foreign lands he had visited that the boy agreed.

Caleb's home consisted of one large room and a porch. A table, a couple of chairs, a bed, and a fireplace where he did his cooking were all the furnishings he had. Entering the room, the boy flopped into a chair and watched the sailor tidying the place a bit.

"I don't think I would care for coconut," he blurted out.

"What do you like?" Caleb asked.

The boy pursed his lips, then said, "Apple dumplings swimming in sugar sauce, huge rice puddings, muffins, biscuits, like I see sometimes in the house next to ours."

"Doesn't your grandmother make any of those things for you?"

"She?" the boy said with a sneer.

Caleb smiled. "I gather you aren't exactly fond of your grandparents, John. Why?"

Ignoring the question, John said "You promised to tell me about faraway lands."

Caleb readily agreed. He told the boy about the mysteries of the sea and the fantastic fish living in its depths, about islands more beautiful than any lands in fairy tales. He did everything to keep the restless boy from leaving. Toward evening he took him back to his grandparents.

The whole of that day there had been no disturbance in the cobbler's house. Nor were there any flying objects whirling around the room the next day and the day that followed.

Then it started up again. One night Morse

and his wife were in bed asleep when a rattling noise woke them up. Believing it to be coming from outside, they went out to see what caused it. Although there seemed to be no one there, stones and sticks kept pounding against the roof and sides of the house as if hurled by an invisible hand. Terrified, they ran back into the house and locked the door. After a while the fearful noise subsided, but no sooner had they decided to go back to bed when they heard footsteps in the house.

"I'll get that evil spirit if that's the last thing I do," Morse declared and, grabbing a poker, ran downstairs. What he saw was so unexpected that he stopped short, rubbing the back of his head, perplexed. His pig roaming about the room! He knew he had bolted the door — then how had it gotten in? "Out with you, you dirty swine!" he shouted. It was only when the pig scrambled for the door that he noticed it was half open.

Morse and his wife, brooding over their misfortune, couldn't fall asleep for a long while. At last he said, "The more I think of it, the more I'm convinced it's that sailor, Caleb Powell. He must be a wizard. He must be the one turning the evil spirit on and off. I can't explain it otherwise."

"That's what I think," his wife echoed.

"Maybe we should complain to the judges."

Rumors that the cobbler's house was be-witched had been going around town for some time. Now the townspeople learned from Morse himself that Caleb Powell, posing as a kindly neighbor, was in fact a wizard and the one re-sponsible for all the devilish mischief. Many in-dignantly insisted this must be stopped. Soon Caleb Powell was arrested and brought to court.

Caleb Powell's trial was held in March 1680 before three judges in the nearby town of Ip-swich. William Morse was called as the chief witness against Caleb Powell. After recounting all the misery inflicted upon him, Morse pointed at Powell and declared, "He's the one. He's a wizard, that I'm sure of. I can prove it." He paused to catch his breath and then con-tinued, "He came to me one day and claimed he was sorry for me. Then he said if I'd let him have the boy just for one day I'd have no more trou-ble. Against my best judgment, I agreed. And, as he foretold, I had no trouble for a few days. Then he started it again, this wizard I mean."

Two other witnesses testified they had often overheard a shipmate of Powell's saying that if there were wizards, Caleb Powell surely was one.

However, a young girl, Mary Tucker, took his

side. Caleb, she told the court, had come to her house and told her that passing William Morse's house, he had looked into the window and clearly seen the boy hiding under a chair and throwing shoes at his grandfather. Maybe the boy was doing it because he thought he was being mistreated, Caleb had explained to her.

"What can you say in your own defense?" one of the three judges asked Powell.

Scratching the back of his head, Caleb took time to reply. "All I can say is that I truly tried to help my neighbor, and for that good deed he's now accusing me of being a wizard."

After carefully studying the case against Powell, the court came to the following conclusion: "There is not enough evidence to convict Caleb Powell of being a wizard. However, there is enough ground for suspicion that he may have been dealing with the Devil. Therefore his only punishment shall be that he bears his own shame and the costs of the trial."

Soon after he was set free, Caleb Powell got an assignment on a ship sailing for Europe. He carried no grudge against William Morse. But before leaving, he sought out the boy. "Let me give you a bit of advice, John Stiles," he told him sternly. "You know I'm suspected of being a wizard. Maybe I am at that. Now you'd better behave yourself or else I'll put you on the back of a dolphin who'll carry you across all the seas until it finds a shark large enough to swallow you whole. There in the dark you'll have to spend the rest of your life."

The cobbler William Morse and his wife were never troubled by evil spirits again.

Voices in the Night

Thomas Tracy, the tailor of Wethersfield, Connecticut, was having a bad day, and he blamed it all on his neighbor Katherine Harrison. He didn't know whether it was the evil spirit in her that had prompted the quarrel with his good friend when he refused to lend him his horse saddle. But it was odd that she should have been passing his house soon afterward. It was also strange that, experienced a tailor as he was, he suddenly couldn't sew a single stitch right. No matter how many times he tried to fit the sleeves into the jacket he was making, he would find that he had placed them wrongly and had to rip them out again. And when he cut the cloth for breeches, he was dismayed to find that the two sides of the breeches were of completely different colors. All this was befuddling, especially since normally he did things right.

Later on in the day, feeling a need for fresh air, he stepped out of the house, and what he saw made him shudder. A haycart was moving toward Katherine Harrison's shed, and on top of it was a bright red calf's head with its ears perked up. Before his eyes the calf's head disappeared, and for a moment Katherine's dead husband appeared in its place and then vanished.

"Witch, I know you're a witch! I just saw you work your evil!" he shouted wildly. He saw her coming toward him, but he remained standing where he was as if his feet were glued to the ground.

"Neighbor, you aren't in your right mind. You need a good rest," she told him calmly.

"Witch, everybody knows you're a witch," he went on shouting.

"Stop this slander, or I'll make you stop," she warned him.

Thomas watched her going back to her house and shook his fist scornfully. She couldn't frighten him with her threats, he thought, and she couldn't make a fool out of him; he was in excellent health and had all his senses.

Nevertheless he went to bed early. But he was abruptly awakened by the sound of voices.

Standing at his bedside were the friend he had quarreled with and Katherine. He could clearly hear them arguing about how to put an end to him. His friend wanted to use the knife he was holding, but Katherine held him back, insisting that choking would be better and that she should be given the pleasure of watching him suffer for a while.

Suddenly a string was around his neck, pulling and pinching him. The pain became so unbearable that he couldn't hold back his moans. Fortunately his father heard his moans and, rushing over to his bed, asked what the trouble was. Immediately Katherine and his friend let go of him. But shortly after his father left, Katherine started in once more, forcing him to groan again.

Exhausted by the night's torture, Thomas stayed in bed the following day. But the news of Katherine's evil work spread rapidly among the neighbors. That afternoon Katherine found her horse lying with a broken back in the meadow.

"Is there no sanity left on earth?" Katherine lamented. This was not the first time harm had been done to her animals. Only a month before, the earmark on one of her cows had been cut out and someone else's mark set in.

She was aware that the neighbors were envious and suspicious of her. Only recently she had overheard them whispering, "The way she tells fortunes, she must be guided by the Devil. She's a Sabbath-breaker too. And how could any woman appear so fresh and lively after a hard day's work? It's unnatural!" True, she liked to amuse herself telling people's fortunes after first learning their past, the way the clever fortune-teller Mr. Lilley had taught her to do. The fools; because of such trifles they thought she was a witch.

Thomas Tracy stayed in bed four days and didn't go back to work for a while after that. Seeing him sitting on his stoop looking weak, his neighbors stopped to talk to him.

"How are you getting on?" farmer Dickinson inquired. "I hope your affliction has left you."

"I'll be all right," Thomas assured him.

"I just came upon this Katherine Harrison," farmer Montague revealed, joining them. "You know what she said to me? She told me that a swarm of her bees had flown away over the meadow and across the river, but she instantly fetched them back again. Now I don't see how she could have done such an amazing feat without the help of the Devil."

"She couldn't have done it any other way," Dickinson agreed. "I also saw her on the meadow the other day. 'Hoccanum! Hoccanum! I heard her calling. I looked around, and there were her cows at least a mile away. The cows were surely too far to hear her call, yet they came running like crazy with their tails on end. Peculiar, isn't it?"

At that moment Mary Hale came walking along the road.

"She walks perky, doesn't she? There's a girl who'd make you a good wife, Thomas," Dickinson said, nodding his head meaningfully.

However, Mary wasn't feeling as well as she appeared to farmer Dickinson, and as the day wore on she could hardly drag herself to bed. Her worried parents kept the fire ablaze in the fireplace to make the room both warm and bright for her.

Mary was certain she wasn't asleep when she heard a sound as if someone were opening the door of her room. She moved her eyes in that direction, but light as the room was, she could see no one entering. All at once something landed on her legs, and the pain was so terrible that she was afraid she would never be able to use them again. No sooner did the pain in her legs ease somewhat when something began to press on her stomach and chest, causing her to gasp for breath.

What can it be? she wondered, wildly looking

about the room. Ah, there it was, an ugly-shaped dog with a face closely resembling Katherine Harrison's! Too stunned to scream, she saw it scurrying about the room, stopping at her parents' bed, then disappearing.

The following night Mary felt the same pains again. As she put her hand on her chest, trying to ease the pain, her fingers touched a face. Then she heard a voice, "Do you not fear me?"

"No," Mary replied. "I'm not afraid of you."

"I will make you afraid before I am done with you," the voice said.

As the pressure on her body increased, Mary tried to call to her father and mother sleeping in the same room, but no sound came out of her mouth.

"No use calling them; they won't hear you till after I am gone," the voice cautioned her. "You made a wish that they should carry me to the gallows in my own cart, didn't you?"

"How do you know that? I told this to no one except my mother."

"That is why I brought such affliction upon you," the voice said.

"The Devil must have sent you!" Mary cried out.

"No," the voice whispered in her ear. "I came by God's will. Now, if you promise to keep my visit a secret I won't afflict you any more."

"I won't promise," Mary retorted. "You can't fool me, Katherine Harrison; I know who you are."

"Think it over," the voice warned her. With that it vanished into the night.

Mary was confined to bed for three weeks, blaming it on the fact that she hadn't kept the night visit a secret. Hearing her tale, Thomas Tracy exclaimed, "I had the same affliction as you did. And it was that cursed witch Katherine who brought it on me!"

When the villagers heard about Katherine's evil doings, they decided it was time to do something about it. Soon afterward Katherine Harrison was seized, taken to jail, and summoned for trial in Hartford.

The court was packed with people whose tension showed on their faces as they listened to the judge reading to the prisoner:

"Katherine Harrison, you are accused of being guilty of witchcraft, of having no fear of God and being familiar with Satan, the greatest enemy of God and all mankind. That with the help of Satan you have been inflicting body injuries on innocent people which, according to the law, is punishable by death."

Pleading not guilty, Katherine asked to be

tried by a jury. To the great disappointment of the crowd, who had expected instant excitement, her request was granted.

Losing no time, Katherine submitted a set of her own complaints to the court. For the last two years, since she had become a widow, she had been constantly harassed, and her animals injured or killed by some of the people in Wethersfield. One time her yoke of oxen, while standing right at her house, were assaulted by blows on their backs and sides. Her horse had been injured in the same manner. Another time her brand marks on her heifer and sow had been cut out and others set in. Her cornfield had been trampled by horses and sacks of wheat spilled all over the yard. For these damages and many more she could give the court all the proof needed.

A few months later the trial of Katherine Harrison was finally resumed. Many witnesses were called to testify against the accused, among them Thomas Tracy and Mary Hale. Then on the twelfth of October 1669 the jury pronounced their verdict: Katherine Harrison was guilty of witchcraft. Many among those present at the trial were jubilant. "Give the witch what she deserves — hang her!" they clamored.

However, the magistrates had nagging doubts whether the accused had really been given a fair verdict. Could it be possible that the testimony the witnesses had given was merely the outcome of imagination, or of spite? Thomas Tracy may have been convinced that his tale about Katherine Harrison's night visit and her threats to choke him were true. But wasn't Tracy suffering from a high fever at that time? It was peculiar that his parents, who came to his bedside when he groaned, were not aware of a stranger's being in the room. And how true was Mary Hale's tale? Was she in her right mind when she saw the shape of a dog with a human head resembling Katherine Harrison's? At any rate only she alone had seen it; there was no one else who could verify her story.

In order to dispel their doubts, the magistrates consulted not only the laws of Connecticut but even the gospel. They finally came to the conclusion that any evidence presented by a witness against the accused must be sworn to by at least one more person if it is to be accepted as a fact. With this in mind, they sent Katherine Harrison's case and their final judgment to a special court of assistance for reconsideration.

After studying the case, the court of assistance pronounced the jury's verdict unfair. They ordered Katherine Harrison to be released from prison and set free after she paid the court expenses. There was another condition she had to agree to. "For your own safety and for the sake of your neighbors' peace of mind you must move away from Wethersfield," she was told.

Katherine's joy at being declared innocent gave way to indignation as she realized that she must leave the home where she had spent a good part of her life. But then she remembered how terrible things had been of late. Comforting herself with a promise of better times, she moved to Westchester, New York. Even there the suspicion that she was a witch pursued her. But finally she was left alone to live out her days in peace.

The Ghosts of Gibbet Island

Before the Revolutionary War, a little island in New York harbor, near where the Hudson River flows into the ocean, was the setting for grim happenings. People dared to speak of the place only in whispers and called it fittingly Gibbet Island. For captured pirates, bound in chains, were hauled there and hung from the gallows.

In sharp contrast was the way people spoke about the peaceful village of Communipaw, just across the water from Gibbet Island. It was a model of pleasant community life, and its Dutch settlers, with the help of the English authorities, did all they could to keep it that way. Their special pride was Wild Goose Tavern, with its sign of a painted goose hanging by the entrance.

There they came to spend their leisure time, smoking their pipes, drinking Dutch Courage, and meeting their friends. That was until strange things began to happen.

One day a Dutch merchant, sitting in the tavern with a group of friends, was amusing them with tales about the antics and peculiar humor of the Yankees he had met during his travels. While enjoying spinning his tales, the Dutchman reached for the pipe he had laid down on the table. But as he tried to light it, he was seized with a frightful fit of sneezing. Emptying his pipe, he discovered that it had been mysteriously refilled with snuff tobacco.

"Must be that brat Vanderscamp. He needs to have his ears boxed," one of the company declared.

It happened that the following evening a fur trader, who had been away trading with the Indians, showed up at the tavern. Feeling in a generous mood, he treated everybody to drinks. As the evening progressed, the gay and friendly company noisily proclaimed that he was one grand fellow. At last, wishing them all a good night, he went out to mount his horse. To his surprise, his usually friendly animal jumped and pranced, and no amount of patting and soothing could induce it to let him mount. Finally, noticing that his horse was slashing its tail as if trying to chase away some stinging bugs, he got hold of the tail to see what was wrong. What he found made him gnash his teeth: under the tail was a clump of rosebush thorns.

"Who else but that brat Vanderscamp would play such a mean prank," he raged as he removed the prickly clump. Resolving to warn the boy's uncle that he must restrain his nephew if he didn't want to lose all his customers, he mounted his horse and rode away cursing.

However, neither his uncle, who owned the tavern, nor anyone else could make Van Yost Vanderscamp behave. He listened to his uncle's admonitions with the eyes of an innocent puppy and then went on playing his pranks as usual.

When his uncle died, Vanderscamp became the owner of the Wild Goose. He was now a strong and wiry young man with a quick mind and a clever tongue. Eager for adventure and not satisfied with merely managing the tavern, he gathered around him a group of daredevils and proclaimed himself their leader. No passing ship was safe from Vanderscamp's gang of pirates. They hid their plunder in the Wild Goose, and celebrated their hauls with drink, song, and wild parties.

"It is bad enough that we can no longer go to the Wild Goose, but the tavern has become a disgrace to our village," the people complained to the English authorities, and urged them to get rid of the pirates.

Hearing about the villagers' complaint, Vanderscamp's servant and ally, Pluto, cautioned him to be careful.

"Afraid of the flatfooted redcoats? Not me!" Vanderscamp sneered, and ordered his gang to get ready to sail.

They sailed back and forth along the coast looking for suitable prey. A three-masted schooner appeared and passed close by, but though they were tempted, it was too large to challenge. A while later they met with a few fishing boats and, as such boats promised little in the way of booty, they also let them pass. Finally sighting a sloop on the horizon, they waited, then sent their boat headlong toward the ship as if they were going to ram it. But at the last moment they whirled their boat around, pulling it up smartly alongside the sloop.

Vanderscamp and his daredevils lost no time boarding the ship and attacking its crew. The fight was fierce but short. After subduing the crew, the pirates collected whatever valuables there were and transferred them to their own boat. Then they punched a hole in the sloop's side and left it to its fate. As always, they waited till dark to unload their spoils.

Meanwhile the news of another pirate attack reached the people of Communipaw. "Must be that rascal Vanderscamp and his band," they cried.

The sky was starless and the villagers had long gone to sleep when the pirates began to unload their booty. In the midst of the unloading, Vanderscamp thought he heard a suspicious rustling in the bushes and motioned to his men to stop. Peering into the darkness, he spied the glint of a red coat and signaled danger to his crew. Dropping their haul, the pirates scrambled in all directions. The redcoats, rushing out of hiding, tried to trap them, but they escaped under the covering darkness — all except three. Determined to get Vanderscamp, the redcoats hurried to the Wild Goose and knocked at the door.

After a while the door opened slightly and Pluto's head appeared. "What do you want?"

"Where is Vanderscamp?" they demanded.

"He is asleep."

Taken aback, the redcoats exchanged puzzled glances. "Asleep? Since when?" one of them asked.

"I don't know," Pluto shrugged. "He had his dinner and went right to bed."

"You are lying," the redcoat barked. "Take us to him."

Resignedly Pluto unbarred the door and led them to the room where Vanderscamp, in a nightshirt and cap, was lying sprawled on his bed, seemingly fast asleep.

"Well, well," the redcoat declared, scratching his head. As they were leaving the Wild Goose, he grumbled to the others, "He thinks he is too clever for us, but one of these days we'll catch him with the goods."

The three swashbuckling ruffians the redcoats did capture were put in prison. A quick trial followed, then they were taken to Gibbet Island in chains, and were promptly hanged.

"We'd better leave the Wild Goose; it's no longer safe here," Pluto cautioned Vanderscamp.

But the pirate leader shrugged that off. "Three men more or less don't matter. There's no cause for alarm."

A few days later, Vanderscamp was told about an old ship stranded not far off shore. His curiosity aroused, he asked Pluto to row out with him to see whether the ship was worth plundering.

Pluto hesitated. "That might be a bit too risky now."

"Don't be a milksop. It's only an innocent boat ride," Vanderscamp replied.

The weather changed for the worse as they

rowed out to sea, but Vanderscamp paid no attention to it. They found nothing of value on the stranded ship.

"It's getting late, and look at the threatening sky," Pluto kept reminding him.

Not heeding the warning, Vanderscamp went on searching the ship, refusing to believe there was no hidden treasure. Darkness had descended when he finally gave up his search. As they started back to the Wild Goose, thunder and lightning broke over the sea, the water turned black, and rain fell in sheets. High waves tipped with whitecaps dashed against the boat, pushing it off course toward Gibbet Island.

Louder than the wind and louder than the wash of waves came a strange noise — clank ...grind, clank...grind....

"What's that?" Vanderscamp shouted, but the roar of the sea and the eerie grinding noise drowned out his words. "Where's that coming from?" he shouted with all his might.

Pointing at the sky, Pluto shouted back, "Look!"

Vanderscamp looked up and for the first time in his life trembled with fear. Above swayed his three friends — hanging ropes around their necks, their rags flapping, their chains grinding in the wind!

"Aren't you glad to see your friends? Surely

the brave leader is not afraid of dead men!"
Pluto taunted.

Jumping to his feet, Vanderscamp screamed,
"Me, fear them?" Bowing to the dangling
pirates, he shouted, "Hail, my wind-swinging
friends! Come to supper at the Wild Goose
whenever the fancy takes you!"

The wind suddenly swirled the boat around
and pushed it away from the island. It was midnight when they at last reached Communipaw.
Drenched and chilled, Vanderscamp left Pluto
to take care of the boat and hurried to the Wild
Goose. His nerves on edge, he had difficulty unlocking the door. The tavern was dark and no
one was on the main floor, but plainly coming
from the room above was the noise of a wild
party.

"The rascals, how the devil did they get in?"
Vanderscamp growled and, rushing upstairs,
flung open the door.

Around a table loaded with food and drink
and lit by the weird blue flicker of candles sat
the three pirates of Gibbet Island. Lifting their
tankards, they were singing at the top of their
hoarse voices. Noticing Vanderscamp, they fo-
cused their glassy eyes on him!

"Hail, old faithful friend! Welcome to our
party!" they called.

With a wild glance Vanderscamp took in their

death-white faces, the nooses around their necks, and the chains on their feet.

"Come in, come in! Don't be afraid of your friends!" they insisted, filling the room with hollow laughter.

Speechless and horror-stricken, Vanderscamp backed away from the door. In his panic he missed a step, fell headlong down the stairs, and was killed instantly.

Once he was gone, the Wild Goose closed and never reopened. Without their leader the gang of pirates disbanded, and the village became peaceful again.

But for a long time afterward, boatmen would tell strange tales of seeing pirates floating over Gibbet Island, cursing, clanking their chains, and carrying on as though they didn't know they were dead.

Years later Gibbet Island was renamed Ellis Island. However, the strange tales about this haunted isle persisted, and boatmen carefully avoided coming too close to it after dark.

The Evil Eye

During the years when California was a Spanish colony, the early settlers never succeeded in gaining the goodwill of their neighbors, the Indians. Claiming the Spaniards were intruders, the Indians constantly plotted against them and harassed them whenever they could.

Hermenegildo Salvatierra was not only an efficient Governor of California, but a brave man who often marched out with his soldiers to teach the unruly Indians a lesson in good behavior. In one of the skirmishes the Governor single-handedly felled seven Indians. However, as he turned to finish the last one, an arrow struck him, shooting out his right eye.

With the loss of his eye not merely did the Governor's appearance change, but also his whole character. Up to then he had kept himself aloof and was ruthless to his subjects when they didn't obey his orders. Now his manner became gentler, his voice friendlier, and his face with the darkened eye shone with a kindness the people had never seen before. They came to him for all sorts of advice: Men asked how to deal with a troublesome neighbor or how to treat an ailing horse, and women, dragging their naughty children along, wanted to know how to make them behave. The good Governor had time and advice for everyone.

One rainy afternoon in 1797 the Governor was sitting alone before his fireplace, gazing with his sound eye into the fire as though expecting something to happen.

"Captain Peleg Scudder of the schooner *General Court* from Salem, Massachusetts," his attendant announced, ushering in a stocky man with a weather-beaten face, and wearing a sou'wester.

"Ah, my friend!" the Governor exclaimed, rushing over and embracing the visitor. Then turning to his attendant, he commanded, "Bring the finest wine I have in the cellar. And tell the cook to prepare a feast for my excellent friend."

"But he is a Yankee," the attendant objected, giving the visitor a hostile glance.

"I know, but do as I say," the Governor ordered hm.

When they were seated and the wine was brought, the Governor said, "Now, Captain, tell me about your journey to the Far East."

Between rounds of drinking to each other's good health, the Captain from Salem told the Governor about the curious races of people he had met, their customs, their gods and temples, so different from those in the Western countries. Too bad Yankees were not permitted to stay awhile in California, for he would have liked to show him all the amazing silks, cotton goods, teakwood, and ebony carvings he had brought back with him.

With each bowl of wine they drank, the Governor's friendship for the Captain increased in tenderness. By the time they had finished their fourth bowl, the Governor, for want of the right words, burst into song. And when their fifth bowl was emptied, he insisted that his Yankee friend get up on the table with him. Then with a flourish he proceeded to teach him how to dance the Spanish cachucha.

The revelry went on till late hours of the night. For it was a rare event when so good a friend as Captain Scudder, Yankee though he was, stopped at the shores of California on his return from the Far East.

The next day the Governor appeared before his astonished people with a right eye. Hearing of this, the priests came running and stood gazing in awe at the Governor. "A miracle!" they breathed, then went back to their churches to offer special services for the marvelous happening. Church bells rang out and a three-day holiday was declared. People from every part of California came pouring in to get a glimpse of the Governor's right eye for themselves. "It's even nicer shaped than the left one!" they all proclaimed after seeing it. They drank to the health of their amazing Governor, joined the throngs dancing in the open air, and watched the games especially arranged in honor of this occasion.

Some of the priests, losing no time, went off to tell the red men in the vicinity about the miracle that had happened to the Governor, pointing out to them what praying and faith could do.

Mothers suddenly discovered a way of making their children behave by telling them that wonderful things would happen to them if they kept on being good and obeyed their parents.

But no one was happier than Governor Salvatierra, as he moved with his head raised high among the cheering crowd.

During their rejoicing the people didn't notice anything unusual about the Governor's right eye. However, as time passed some began to wonder about it.

One day as a dry-goods merchant was measuring out a length of material for a customer, the Governor happened to come by and stopped to watch. Lifting his head from his work to greet him, the merchant was taken aback by the Governor's right eye staring at him as though piercing through him. Did the Governor mean to accuse him of selling foreign material prohibited by law? No one in California was obeying that law, and the Governor knew it. Then why was he singling him out to blame? Shrinking under the Governor's persistent stare, the merchant stammered, "I know, I know. I promise to obey the law in the future."

"I am glad you are aware of it," the Governor said.

As soon as the Governor walked off, the merchant hurried to share his strange experience with other merchants. They listened with grave faces and shook their heads, unable to offer any explanation.

A few days later the candlemaker of the settlement was busily dipping a row of cotton wicks suspended from a frame into hot tallow, lifting them out to cool, and dipping them again. Suddenly he became aware of the Governor's presence. "Good afternoon, your lordship!" the candlemaker greeted him. His glad smile vanished as he met the Governor's cold steady stare.

Terrified, he tried to back away. He heard the Governor saying, "Fine candles you are making," but it gave him no comfort. It was that stare! He was sure it really meant, "Where did you get the tallow?" Against his will he said aloud, "I didn't know the tallow came from stolen cattle."

"I believe you," the Governor replied. But the cold stare of his right eye didn't seem to agree with what he was saying.

For a while, after the Governor left, the candlemaker remained standing, wiping the sweat off his forehead. Later on he told his wife, "I wonder how much good the miracle really did the Governor. It certainly didn't do us any good."

It happened, soon after, that one of the baker's boys, delivering a basket of bread to the Governor's house, saw the Governor entering the kitchen. He noticed with astonishment that as the Governor spoke pleasant words to the cook, the lower part of his face seemed to be smiling while the upper part remained serious. Excited over this discovery, he ran to tell other boys about it. Soon faces were peeping out from behind bushes and doorways eager to get a good look at the passing Governor.

While the boys were merely curious, the older people began to worry about the Governor's miraculous eye. Whispers soon spread around that it was really an evil eye, that it could penetrate and reveal the deepest thoughts of men and make them confess their most guarded sins. The people came to fear the eye. Some even insisted that the Governor must be in league with the Devil.

Sensing how people felt about him, the Governor changed back to the stern mistrustful ruler he had formerly been. However, he didn't suspect where all this trouble stemmed from.

The Indians in the nearby mission now feared the Governor more than they had in the past. They appealed to their elders to tell them what to do.

"The root of our trouble is that evil eye. We must destroy it," the elders told them.

"I will go," one of the braves declared.

The full moon was spreading a silvery light over the land as the brave, crawling on his stomach, stole his way to the Governor's home. The night being warm, the tall windows facing the garden were wide open, and the moon shining through them cast light on the sleeping Governor. Noiselessly the brave stepped into the room and tiptoed to the bedside. But as he bent over to take a good look at the face of the sleeping man, he was seized with horror. While the left eye was fast asleep, the right one was fully awake, fixing him with an evil stare. Falling back, he let out a howl that roused the Governor.

Realizing that there was a prowler in the room, the Governor jumped out of bed, grabbed a stiletto, and went after him. For a time they were locked in a violent struggle, neither one giving ground. At the end the Governor got the upper hand, and the Indian had to flee to save his life. However, the Governor didn't come out of the fight unharmed. A jab he could not avoid landed on his right eye with tremendous force, knocking it out.

Great was the people's joy when they saw the Governor with his right eye darkened again. "Thank the Lord, the evil eye has left him!" they kept telling each other. They now greeted the Governor as though he were an old friend who had just returned from a hazardous journey. No longer frightened by the malevolent stare of his eye, they again came to him with their troubles for his wise counsel. And he, now realizing the cause of their fright, responded like a forgiving father, with kindness and understanding. He never had the heart to reveal the truth to them — that his supposed evil eye was really a glass eye brought to him from the Far East by his Yankee friend.

The Ghost That Came to Stay

Betsy Bell was fifteen when a mysterious guest came to live in her house. Who this invisible visitor was and what it wanted, no one seemed to know. The uninvited guest couldn't have chosen a nicer family or a pleasanter home. Betsy's father was well-respected in the community, and as for her mother, there was no woman more likable than she. Her two older brothers, John Jr. and Drew, were always filling the house with gaiety and laughter.

But it was Betsy, with her intelligent blue eyes, long blond hair, and gracious ways, who was the center of attraction in the Bell family. That she was beautiful, she must have known by the timidly admiring glances boys would cast at her. Particularly attentive was Joshua Gordon, the son of a wealthy neighbor whose land adjoined Bell's farm. A sedate youth with proper manners, Joshua was her father's favorite among the young people. Although Betsy seemed agreeable to her father's choice, no one really knew what she thought about this or anything else.

One thing Betsy did say about her father was that he was an enterprising man. He had not hesitated to leave North Carolina back in 1804 and follow the tide of settlers who had gone to Tennessee, seeking good land with plenty of water and timber. Coming to Robertson County in his horse-driven wagon laden with his young family and a number of slaves, he had purchased the large farm, the orchard, and the house they were now living in.

It was after Betsy's two brothers returned home from a trip to New Orleans, where they visited distant relatives, that the mysterious guest came to stay.

One evening when Mr. Bell was settled in his comfortable chair, enjoying his after-supper pipe with his wife contentedly sewing nearby, they were suddenly startled by loud knocking on the door and walls. Flinging open the door, Mr. Bell saw no one there. As they were about to settle down again, they heard terrified screaming coming from Betsy's room.

Rushing upstairs,they found Betsy huddled in a corner holding onto her hair, still screaming. "It slapped my face! It's pulling my hair! It's after me!"

"Quiet down! Tell us who is after you," her father demanded.

"I — I don't know," Betsy stammered.

Just then the boys came running in. Learning what had happened, they set about searching the room but turned up nothing.

Putting her arms around Betsy, her mother said soothingly, "I'm sure nothing more will happen. Let's all try to get some rest."

However, the following evening the mysterious presence gave them no peace. No sooner did the knocking on the walls and door leave off, than a persistent scratching in the boys' room began. Exhausted from trying to track down the source of the turmoil, the family finally retired. But in the middle of the night the parents were startled awake by a tug on their blanket, and could only watch in bewilderment as it was whisked off the bed by unseen hands. As night after night the disturbances were repeated, Mr. Bell finally decided to call in his neighbors for help.

Eager to unravel the mystery, his friends

came flocking to the house. One of them, James Johnson, a plump and kindly man, turned to Betsy and said, "Poor girl, you got the harshest treatment. Must be a spirit doing it. Do you think it is in the room now and can hear us?"

"Perhaps," Betsy muttered, and with a shrug left the room.

While the visitors were exchanging puzzled glances, Johnson, staring into space, raised his voice. "We cannot see you; can you see us? Prove it. How many are we?"

Quickly ten knocks came in reply.

Encouraged, Johnson continued, "Now, let us hear your voice."

The invisible presence said nothing. But when Betsy returned to the room, to everyone's astonishment it suddenly spoke up.

"I live in the woods, in the air, in the water, in houses with people. I live in heaven and hell. I am all things and anything I want to be. Now, don't you know what I am?"

"It's a ghost," the whisper went around the room.

Shushing everyone, Johnson offered a prayer, read from the Bible, and sang a hymn. "That should do it," he declared confidently.

Immediately the spirit voice began mimicking word for word Johnson's performance. The imitation was so perfect that the company turned to him to see if his lips were moving. But Johnson, equally flabbergasted, just sat with his mouth open.

While they were sitting speechless, Joshua Gordon came in. As he started to cross the room toward Betsy, the spirit cried out, "Hear me, Betsy Bell: Don't ever marry Joshua Gordon."

Indignantly, Betsy's father hurled back, "Joshua is a fine boy; she shall marry him."

"Don't marry Joshua...." the voice repeated.

As the company could coax nothing more from the spirit, they decided to leave. Standing at the door, Betsy's brother Drew pleaded, "Please come again. Maybe we'll have better luck next time."

Soon Bell's friends assembled in his house again to make another try. One after another called out to the ghost, "What do you want? Reveal yourself!"

"Listen well," the voice spoke. "I am the spirit of an early settler. Nearby, there is a fortune which I buried but revealed to no one while I lived. I cannot rest until my mission is done.

"Hear me and do my bidding. You, Drew, and your friend Bennett Potter, go to the southwest corner of the farm. There, at the mouth of the spring under a stone, you will find my treasure. Mind you, every penny must go to Betsy Bell. I appoint you, 'Old Sugar Mouth' Johnson, to supervise the digging and see that my instructions are carried out."

Drew and Bennett armed themselves with shovels and spades and hurried to the spot, followed by Johnson. After hours of strenuous shoveling, pushing, and heaving, they managed to remove the large stone. Finding nothing, they desperately dug a hole to the depth of six feet. Failing to spot a trace of treasure, they gave up in disgust.

As soon as they entered the house they shouted to the spirit, "What kind of fool's errand did you send us on?"

A burst of gleeful laughter was the only answer.

"Is there really any money hidden away?" they demanded.

"A clever trick, wasn't it?" the ghost chuckled.

"The Devil take you," Johnson grumbled, and quit the house.

The one most upset at the ghost's persistent presence was John Bell. Feeling that he was no longer master in his own house, he kept dwelling on what he could do to get rid of the intruder.

Aware of his friend's concern, Johnson said to him one day, "I know a conjurer in Franklin, Kentucky — Dr. Mize by name. Maybe he can help you to get rid of the ghost."

Grudgingly Bell consented, and Dr. Mize was sent for. The conjurer arrived with bags full of flasks and chemicals, ready to attempt to banish the ghost. He waited for some sign of the spirit's presence, but days passed and the house remained perfectly peaceful.

"Ghosts are always afraid of me," Dr. Mize boasted. To pass the time he entertained the visitors with his magic tricks.

One afternoon Mize was busily mixing some chemicals to perform a magic trick for the gathered people, when unexpectedly the mysterious voice spoke up, "Are you sure you know what you are doing?"

Startled, the conjurer looked around but saw nothing. "You left out an important chemical from your charm mixture," the voice persisted.

Confused, Dr. Mize found himself asking, "What did I leave out?"

"Don't ask silly questions. If you can't even perform a magic trick properly, how do you expect to form a cloud and make me appear in it?"

"How do you know what I was about to do?" Mize demanded angrily.

"You are a silly goose," the voice replied, laughing.

Throwing up his hands, Mize turned to Bell. "I've had enough. I'm leaving."

After the ghost had put the conjurer to flight,

it became more of a busybody than ever. There was hardly a secret or a happening in the neighborhood that the spirit wasn't ready to talk about. Anyone who swore too heartily, told too many lies, or overindulged in whisky had to beware of its sharp tongue. Because the ghost was so outspoken, people started to behave better than they really wanted to.

The tale of the clever ghost spread throughout the region. People on horseback, in carriages, and on foot came flocking to hear its voice. The ghost's fame even reached Nashville, where General Andrew Jackson and his troops were stationed.

"Let's have some fun and ride over to see that ghost or whatever it is," General Jackson told his men.

The following day Jackson and his men on horseback, with a wagon loaded with a tent and provisions, were all on their way to confront the ghost. But as they were nearing Bell's house, though they were traveling on a perfectly smooth road, the wagon suddenly stuck. Dismounting, the men tried to push it while the driver whipped his horses and coaxed them to pull harder. It was useless; the wheels of the wagon remained glued fast to the ground. Finally, General Jackson exclaimed, "By the eternal, men, it must be the ghost!"

Unexpectedly, from somewhere in the bushes lining the road, a sharp metallic voice rang out, "All right, Old Hickory, you can move on with your men now. I'll see you all again tonight."

At that moment the horses started off on their own accord, pulling the wagon as easily as if nothing was wrong.

No longer in the mood for camping out, Jackson and his men went directly to Bell's house to see if they could be put up there. Betsy let them in with a gracious smile and curtsy. Her father, upon hearing who the distinguished visitors were, gladly offered them lodging.

Fatigued though the party was from traveling and the difficulty they had endured on the road, General Jackson insisted on staying up and waiting for the ghost to appear.

When they all were assembled in the living room, which was brightly lit with many candles, one of the men in the General's party drew out a big pistol. Carefully placing a silver bullet in it, he said, "This will discourage any witch or spirit." Holding the pistol at the ready, he began bragging about his many daring successes in tracking down witches and ghosts. Encouraged when the company seemed amused, he went on and on with his tales.

At last the General leaned over to the man next to him and with a twinkle in his eye whispered, "I'll bet that braggart turns out to be a coward. By the eternal, I wish the thing would come; I want to see him run."

The candles were burning low and the flickering lights cast restless shadows on the walls. The company began to tire and drowse. But as Mrs. Bell stood up to order more candles brought in, they were suddenly aroused by the sound of footsteps coming in the room. Then they heard, "All right, Old Hickory, I am ready for business." It was the same metallic voice they had heard on the road.

"Now you, Mr. Smarty with the silver bullet," the voice continued, "here I am, shoot."

"Mr. Smarty" raised his pistol, and aiming at where he thought the voice was coming from, pulled the trigger, but nothing happened.

"Try again," the voice insisted. The man tried again and still the pistol would not shoot. "Now, you old coward, I am going to teach you a lesson," the voice announced.

A resounding slap made the ghost hunter tumble to the ground. Quickly getting back on his feet, he ran around the room like an injured bull, upsetting everything in his way and crying, "My nose! Oh Lord, that Devil has me by the nose!" As the door opened, he dashed out into the night as if pulled by an invisible hand.

Stepping outside, Jackson watched the ghost

hunter capering and yelling. Doubling up with laughter, the General declared that he had never had so much fun in his life.

Joining him in his laughter, the spirit exclaimed, "Watch him go. I'll bet he'll never come back with his old horse pistol. Now, Old Hickory, wait till tomorrow and then I'll show you another rascal in your company."

Although the General was eager to stay on, no one in his company dared risk being the butt of the ghost's pranks. The following morning Jackson reluctantly bid farewell to the hospitable John Bell and his charming daughter Betsy and then led his party back to Nashville.

Months after General Jackson's visit, the invisible guest was still staying on in Bell's house.

One evening Joshua and Betsy were sitting on her lawn, making plans for their future life together, when they were interrupted by the voice. It sounded soft and sad as it pleaded, "Please, Betsy, don't marry Joshua." Seeing that Betsy was terribly upset, Joshua tried to reassure her. But Betsy said resolutely, "I'm afraid for you, Joshua. We can never marry."

Eventually convinced that Betsy was right, Joshua went off to another state. Soon afterward, Betsy married a young schoolteacher whom she had secretly favored for a long time, and went off with him to another part of Tennessee to live a poor but happy life. Her two brothers also married and settled some distance from their parents.

With the young people's departure the ghost finally left the Bell house, and never was its voice heard again.

However, whenever two or more people gathered in the county, a lively argument would start up. "Remember," some argued. "The ghost first appeared after Betsy's two brothers returned from New Orleans. They must have learned ventriloquism there and taught it to their sister. And remember, Betsy was an excellent mimic."

"Nonsense! Betsy was in the room most of the time when we heard the ghost. Also, how would you explain the slapping and pulling a man by the nose?" others argued.

"If Betsy was a ventriloquist, she would be able to throw her voice anywhere in the room without moving her lips. As for her pranks, her brothers must have been in on them," some tried to explain.

And so the debate went on, but the mystery of the ghost who came to stay in the Bell house was never really solved.

The Ghost Challenger

Even before reaching his fourteenth birthday, Tom Caldwell refused to accept without question the fantastic tales his neighbors were telling about evil spirits. He smiled at the oft-told tale of a woman dressed in white appearing just before a misfortune would strike someone in a family. How was it, he argued, that a neighbor who claimed she was visited by this apparition in white continued to remain healthy? And despite all the tongue clucking that something dreadful was bound to happen to someone in her family, nothing did.

One day, hearing that the woman in white had appeared in the vicinity again, Tom decided to play a trick on his brother Allen and his sister Jane. The spacious stone house they lived in with their mother was in the country about fifteen miles from the town of Frederick, Maryland. That the house happened to be near a cemetery didn't bother any of them. Unmindful of the tombstones, they often used it as a playground.

Taller and older than the other children, with unruly hair the color of golden wheat which he kept constantly brushing away from his inquisitive eyes, Tom was their natural leader. On this particular day he encouraged his brother and sister to play in the graveyard longer than usual. When twilight descended, Tom disappeared behind a large tombstone where he had hidden a white sheet. Enfolding himself completely in it, he waited. The moment the children came close to him he jumped out and, imitating the floating motions of a ghost, started after them.

"A spook! A spook!" Allen yelled and, grabbing his little sister by the hand, dragged her away as fast as he could. As they were climbing over the wall, Allen glanced back to see if the ghost was still following them. "There's another one. There are two of them!" he screamed.

Tom turned his head and, horrified, saw what seemed like a real ghost. Hurriedly throwing off his disguise and scaling the wall, he joined his brother and sister in escaping from the ghostly

scene. Back in the safety of their home and somewhat calmed down, he thought, perplexed, "I don't believe in ghosts, yet there it was, chasing after me. Or was it just standing glaring at me? I'm not sure now."

"We'd better not tell Mother or any of the servants what we saw in the graveyard, lest they never let us go there again," he cautioned Allen and Jane.

The next morning they stayed close to home, moving about as if someone in the house were ill. Noticing this, their mother asked, "Why are you all so quiet? What's wrong?"

Allen opened his mouth to answer; but, meeting Tom's warning glance, he merely shrugged his shoulders and muttered, "Nothing."

For a few moments their mother studied them with concern. Then reassured that they were in good health, she said, "My friend Alice and I have to go to Frederick on business. We are leaving at noon and will be back tomorrow. The servants will take good care of you, I am sure." To the old Dutch farmer who had been with them for many years she said, "I trust, Hans, that you will keep an eye on my young ones."

Tom and his brother and sister came along to share the exciting event of seeing their mother and Alice go off on a train journey. Spellbound, they saw the two-car train approach the station and with a terrific thump come to a stop, then, puffing and grinding, start up again. They watched it become smaller and smaller until it disappeared behind the horizon, carrying their mother and Alice away. Reluctant to stay out of doors after their encounter with the ghost the day before, they went directly back to their house.

They had supper early and hurried to the laundry room, where the maids and Hans were spending their leisure time chatting. It was a large room with many doors, one opening to the dining room, another to the kitchen, and one leading to a small hall where the back stairway wound all the way up to the attic.

Seeing the children enter, old Hans grunted expectantly.

"Tell us a story," little Jane demanded, settling herself on the arm of his chair.

The old Dutchman didn't have to be coaxed. Lighting his pipe, he proceeded to tell them about the towns in his country that had canals instead of streets and where homes were built over the water on stilts.

So absorbed were they in what he was saying that they didn't pay any attention to the darkness creeping up into the room.

Suddenly one of the maids motioned frantically to the Dutchman to keep quiet. "Listen!" she whispered.

Everyone in the room strained his ears. But while they couldn't hear any sounds, they sensed that something was gliding into the room through the open door, moving into the dining room, then returning to the laundry room. Whirling several times around them, the "something" glided into the hall. Some thought they could then hear the clatter of hoof beats, others the clank-clank of footsteps ascending the winding stairs.

Somewhat recovering from the scare, old Hans shouted, "Light the lamps!" and ran out of the room. A few moments later he returned, armed with a rusty musket and leading three dogs. Assuming command, he ordered everyone to arm himself with whatever he could find. Scurrying about the room, the maids grabbed brooms, pokers, and shovels. Tom picked up a saber, a memento from the Civil War, Allen a whip, and even Jane grabbed a stick. At a signal from the old Dutchman the whole company dashed into the hall, intent on searching the entire house from cellar to attic.

While they peeped into every corner and behind every piece of furniture, the dogs ran about sniffing. Nothing was overlooked. If they saw a suspicious shadow on the floor, they whacked it with a broom. The sudden flutter of a curtain from an open window prompted them to give the curtain a lusty beating. With a poker and stick, they poked into the clothes hanging in the closets and gave every bed a mighty thumping with brooms and shovels.

"False alarm," Tom declared, after they had finished searching the attic.

That, old Hans denied with a shake of his head. "Something did enter the house. I distinctly heard sounds of footsteps."

"Could have been a mouse or a rat," Tom offered.

"It couldn't be a rat," Hans said decisively. "A rat would go flap-flippety-flap, but this 'something' went clank-clank."

If Hans's declaration didn't convince Tom, it certainly sent an added fright into little Jane. "Let's go to Mother's room — it will be safer there," she pleaded.

Everyone piled into Mrs. Caldwell's room and, huddling together, waited for the night to pass — except the old Dutchman, who remained on guard outside the room with his musket at the ready.

Meanwhile Mrs. Caldwell and her friend Alice, after arriving in Frederick, spent a strenuous afternoon attending to business. Their tedious task finally finished, they went to the City-Hotel intending to stay there overnight and then take the train home in the morning. In the midst of having tea, Mrs. Caldwell said unexpectedly, "I don't know why, but I feel very uneasy about my children."

"Don't you worry; your servants and old Hans are taking good care of them," Alice tried to reassure her.

"I know. Just the same, I have a strange feeling that I shouldn't have left them alone."

"But they are not alone," Alice argued.

For a few moments Mrs. Caldwell remained silent. Then, pushing away her cup, she said resolutely, "I think I will hire a carriage and go home tonight. If you are afraid to take the mountain drive, I will go alone."

"No, I am not afraid," Alice said. "If you insist on going, I will certainly go back with you."

The hotel owner raised his eyebrows when he heard that they wanted to travel at night. "It takes a lot of courage," he declared. Nevertheless, he agreed to find them a reliable driver.

By eight o'clock they were on their way, passing the bridge of Frederick Town close by Barbara Frietchie's house. For a while their thoughts were diverted, remembering the courage of the old woman who not so long before had defied the Confederate troops of Stonewall

Jackson as they entered the town. So staunchly had she refused to draw in the Union flag from her window, that the marching army finally gave in and spared her life and flag.

Leaving Frederick behind them, they were soon traveling in open country. The moon was just rising, and spread a faint light over the land. Here and there they saw the glow of a lighted lamp in a farmhouse, or heard the distant barking of a dog. Despite the rugged dirt road the horses kept up a steady pace, and although the ascent of the Catoctin mountain range was trying, they pushed steadily on. When they reached the top, however, the horses suddenly stopped, backed away snorting, then pulled the carriage downhill with maddening speed.

"What happened?" Mrs. Caldwell asked when at last the driver managed to get the horses under control.

"Something must've frightened them. But don't worry, ma'am, they're all right now," the driver assured her.

It was close to midnight when they passed sleepy Middletown. "Only five miles more," Mrs. Caldwell told Alice hopefully. "We'll be able to see my house from the top of that hill."

The ride up the hill was slow and tedious. The horses kept veering off the road as if something were scaring them. It took the driver much coaxing and skillful maneuvering to make them stay on the road.

"Look, there! A ghost!" Alice suddenly screamed when they reached the top of the hill.

Mrs. Caldwell's face froze with fright. In the distance, glinting in the moonlight, was a figure clad in white. It stood still as if waiting for them.

"Take the side road to the left. And hurry!" Mrs. Caldwell shouted to the driver. To Alice she whispered, "I knew it. I had a premonition."

Mrs. Caldwell avoided looking in the direction where the white ghost was standing and was greatly relieved when the carriage halted safely in front of her house. However, her uneasiness returned as she looked around. "Where are the dogs?" she wondered.

But as she started getting out of the carriage, all the children and the servants along with the dogs came rushing out of the house to meet them.

"Why are you all up so late?" she asked.

"We have a spook in the house," Allen blurted out excitedly.

Tom shooshed him. "Don't listen to him, Mother. It was only a mouse."

"And we just saw a white ghost at the graveyard!" Alice exclaimed.

Giving her friend a disapproving glance, Mrs. Caldwell turned back to the children. "Now, you all go to bed. And don't worry, nothing will happen to you."

That his mother was afraid was obvious to Tom. Why else did she instruct old Hans to stay on guard with his musket all night? Tom remained awake in bed for a long time, the happenings of the past hours whirling in his head. The noise in the house had been caused by a rat; of that he was almost certain. But what about the ghost in the graveyard? Determining to find out more about it, he at last managed to fall asleep.

The following evening, when darkness set in, he stole away on his mission. Climbing over the cemetery wall, he crouched down and waited for the ghost to appear. Something swishing over his head made him shudder, but he immediately realized that it was only a bat. What if the ghost didn't go haunting every night? As Tom pondered what to do, it dawned on him that the tall tombstones ahead of him would prevent him from seeing the ghost even if it did appear. Leaving his hideout, he crawled on his stomach to get in front of them. The full moon had risen high above the horizon and now spread a cool light over the graveyard, etching out each tombstone against the night sky.

As Tom looked up, there was the ghostly something standing in the distance. Leaving himself no time to be frightened, he crawled on among the stones. Pausing to raise his head again, what he saw made him jump to his feet and burst into loud laughter. What appeared from the distance to be a ghost was actually a tree — a silver birch!

Tom could hardly wait till morning to tell everyone in the house what he had discovered.

Allen was first to challenge the truthfulness of his story. "But I saw the ghost — two of them — with my own eyes!" he insisted.

Tom smiled and was about to explain when Alice burst in indignantly, "You mean that whenever someone sees a ghost he really sees a tree?"

Mother too refused to accept his explanation. "Don't ever go to the graveyard alone again, particularly at night," she said sternly.

Tom shrugged his shoulders and went to sit on the stoop. A bee hovering over the flower bed attracted his attention. Watching it move from flower to flower sipping nectar, he thought perhaps in time people, just like this bee, will go about their daily life without seeing ghostly shadows that aren't there. Perhaps someday we'll find answers to all the mysteries.